13
Ways to
Kill Your
Community

13
Ways to
Kill Your
Community

by Doug Griffiths and Kelly Clemmer

Book and cover design: Epix Design
Cover Image: Rick Sealock
Author photos: Ashley Flaade (Doug Griffiths) / Rod Oracheski (Kelly Clemmer)
Editorial assistant: Krista Wiebe

Library and Archives Canada Cataloguing in Publication

Griffiths, Doug
13 ways to kill your community / Doug Griffiths & Kelly Clemmer.

ISBN 978-1-897181-42-3

1. Community development--Canada. 2. Rural development--Canada.
3. Community leadership--Canada.
I. Clemmer, Kelly II. Title. III. Title: Thirteen ways to kill your community.

HN110.Z9C6 2010c   307.1'40971   C2010-904979-9

We acknowledge the support of the Canada Council for the Arts for our publishing program. We also acknowledge the support of The Alberta Foundation for the Arts.

Alberta Foundation for the Arts

Canada Council for the Arts   Conseil des Arts du Canada

Printed and bound in Canada
Published by Frontenac House Ltd.
1138 Frontenac Avenue S.W.
Calgary, Alberta, T2T 1B6, Canada
Tel: 403-245-2491   Fax: 403-245-2380
editor@frontenachouse.com   www.frontenachouse.com

Third printing February 2011

This book is dedicated to the memory of my friend Coady, and those who remain behind, Joanne, Sam, and Nik. We miss you.

Acknowledgements

To the rural communities and wonderful people who shared their stories with me, those that fight tirelessly for the future of their communities; to my family, especially my wife Sue, who supported me always travelling, always being on the road, always talking about the need to keep our communities strong; and to Kelly, who pushed the idea of turning my speech into written word. This book wouldn't have happened without them.
~ Doug Griffiths

I would like to acknowledge my friends and family for all their support, especially my wife, Shannon, son Ashton, and parents Melba and Clare Clemmer for all their encouragement in pursuing my dream of becoming a published author.
~ Kelly Clemmer

Contents

Prologue

I was elected for the first time as a Member of the Legislative Assembly (MLA) of Alberta in the constituency of Wainwright in a by-election on April 8, 2002. I was the youngest MLA serving in the province, and, at the time, the sixth youngest MLA ever elected in the province's 100 year history. I was re-elected to the Legislature for a second term in November, 2004; currently I am well into my third term, which began March, 2008, but thankfully I am no longer the youngest MLA in Alberta, as four new MLAs, all younger than me, were elected this time.

Before becoming a Member of the Legislative Assembly I was a rancher who, like so many other people in our rural communities, also had a career teaching because I truly enjoyed it, and because it subsidized my ranching habit. Before that I received an Honours Degree in Philosophy from the University of Alberta and a collaborative Degree in Education jointly from Red Deer College and the University of Alberta. For three years prior to my first election I taught at Byemoor School, one of the smallest schools in the province, with approximately 50 students from kindergarten through to grade nine. My life was going very well.

Perhaps I should explain a little further. My plan, like that of so many other young people, was to get out of my small town and do some big things in some big places with some big people.

I finished my philosophy studies with the full intent of pursuing a law degree at the University of Alberta. However, when I finished my first degree, I realized I really didn't want to do big things with big people in big cities, and I didn't want to be a lawyer. I wanted to ranch, and I wanted to teach, and I wanted to do these things in a small town because I preferred the small town life. When the University of Alberta partnered with Red Deer College to offer a collaborative teaching degree it meant I could continue to learn, work and live in a small community of my choosing, and I jumped on the opportunity.

There I was, happy as a clam. I grew up on the family farm and I could still work on it. I could still have some cows, and I could still ride my horse. I was teaching in a very small school where the students and staff were exceptional and I was enjoying personal success. When I wasn't working on our farm or teaching, I was taking the students skating, or helping with some work on their family farms, and occasionally dabbling in politics. I had everything I ever wanted.

I recall, however, sitting in the White Goose Restaurant in Castor, Alberta, with a population just under 1,000, on one sunny summer day. I was looking for a house that was well suited and well located for present and future needs, and I was sure it was there, right across the street. Thirty minutes to the south was the school where I would be teaching, and twenty minutes to the east was the farm where I would work after school. But then it struck me as I finished off my second cup of coffee that I wasn't thinking whether this house would be big enough for when I married and had children, or if it had a big enough yard, or had a good foundation, or a nice view. Instead, I wondered if the town I wanted to live in, situated between the town where I taught and the town where I farmed, all three of which I loved so, would still be there as the years went on.

That was the exact moment I had my realization that if I was going to enjoy the life I wanted, if I was going to continue to teach in that small community, continue to farm in the other, and live in the one that lay between the two, it was going to be my responsibility to find a way to make our rural communities stronger, better, and as enduring as time. Eventually I found the woman of my dreams and we had two sons, and the depth of my sense of responsibility and passion grew from being personal to being generational. I wanted, and still want, my sons to be able to grow up in a small town and return someday, if they so desire, just as I did.

So, I became more and more involved in politics, speaking and listening to anyone willing to discuss the issue of rural development and rural sustainability. I wrote columns in newspapers, I wrote letters, and I gave advice to anyone in a position of power who would listen. Then the MLA's position in our constituency fell vacant and I decided to run in the upcoming by-election. Despite a few snickers about my age and some comments that I didn't stand a chance, I ran, and I won. Make no mistake, the irony of giving up my full time rural life, riding my horse and teaching my students, for a life that takes me to the city for extensive periods of time so that I can help ensure that rural communities are prosperous and successful, is not lost on me.

I campaigned in that nomination and in that first election on the need to promote rural development, and though I am in my third term as an elected official, my commitment to rural development is stronger than it has ever been. Soon after I was elected to my first term I was assigned to co-write a rural development strategy for the province. After three years, after visiting over 270 of the 422 communities in Alberta, and after listening to thousands of Albertans, I co-authored a report called *Rural Alberta: the Land of Opportunity*, which listed over 70 recommendations concerning health care, education, community infrastructure, economic development, youth, seniors, Aboriginals, immigrants, arts and culture, the environment, water, transportation, trade, and tourism. The report was well received, which I found gratifying since I had worked long and hard on helping prepare it. I was asked to speak about the report all over the province, and so I did. I always went through all the recommendations, but I also pointed out at the beginning and end of each speech that besides the recommendations, two other elements were critically important.

First, if our rural communities were going to be successful over the long term, it was essential that every level of government realized the role they would need to play in laying down the foundations for success. Whether local, provincial, or federal, each level must be constantly vigilant in pursuing its role in community development. This includes such steps as creating a strong underlying infrastructure, minimizing encumbrances to growth through reduced regulations and paperwork, and developing support systems for exchange of information about best practices.

Second, and most importantly, the only way ever to ensure the success of any community is for the community itself to decide it wants to be successful. I know that sounds trite and banal, but I suggest to you that even the most contentious and complex of challenges often has a very simple solution that we may have overlooked. Perhaps that is because, as intelligent beings, we believe truth must lie in complexity, or perhaps we are just too ashamed that we often cannot recognize the simplest of solutions. Regardless of the situation, a community's future rests primarily within its own populace and their desire to achieve success.

Any government could ride into a community on a white horse with a generic plan and some money to execute that plan, and there might be some short term success within the community. However, if the community members themselves don't write their own plan for success, then they won't truly believe in it as a community and there won't be the commitment to follow through with the plan. This exact scenario happens over and over with programs of this nature, and invariably the plans fall to the wayside and collect dust when the money is gone. In the end, nothing long term has been accomplished and no permanence is achieved, save for a few people who can now feel better about themselves for trying.

So I emphasized in the report itself and with every speech that I gave that without the communities' buy-in, without their own determination, virtually any rural development project would be doomed to failure. Even though the government would follow through on its own recommendations, if the community simply waited for me or anyone else in government to make all their worries and problems go away, then we were all wasting energy. If their notion was that the money that followed the report was the answer and that everything would be just fine with more funding, then we were just wasting taxpayers' money as well. Money is not usually the answer, and it is never the first step in a solution.

Communities have to make a conscious choice if they want to be successful or not. Communities have to analyze their own strengths and weaknesses. Communities have to determine what it is that they can and must do to be successful. Communities have to believe they *can be* successful, and that their plan will make them successful, and they must then follow through on that plan. Communities have to believe that they can achieve their goal with or without government participation.

I travelled all over telling people about the recommendations from the report, about the role of government, and about how first and foremost it was up to the community members themselves to want success. People appreciated the presentation, yet I couldn't help feeling frustrated. I wasn't sure if they got the real message.

I was on my way to one particular community for the third time to give my rural development speech but I was fearful I would get the same reaction. I knew they would do as they had done before. I knew they would love the speech, and listen to the message I emphasized so passionately about their role in making rural development happen, but I knew they would phone me a few weeks after the presentation, as they had done in the past, and ask me when they would see the first benefits from the rural development strategy.

Each time I spoke to them they had missed the point. I can't make them be successful. The government cannot make them be successful. If they themselves don't decide to be successful, if they don't decide to move themselves, to change their own work, there is no amount of money or planning or help that anyone can give them that won't be an exercise in futility. No rules, no legislation, no government, no amount of money, has more impact than a group of people that chooses to make something happen. Conversely, if they *do* decide to make something happen, it's almost impossible to stop them.

You can try to make rules to protect people who make stupid choices, but someone will inevitably make even stupider choices. You can make rules to stop people from hurting themselves but eventually someone will find a new way to hurt themselves despite those rules. You can make laws to try to stop people from losing their fortunes to con artists, yet they will still find a way to give their money away. The government cannot fix every problem that a person has. In fact, I doubt that the government can fix *any* person's problem if the person involved doesn't want to fix it themselves – and if they want to fix it themselves, I doubt very much that they needed the government's help in the first place. It's all about people, the choices they make, and the attitude they have, and it always has been. No matter what happens, the people of the community are the catalysts for its success or failure.

When I was on my way to that community for the third time my frustration grew at the thought of their calling me again to ask when I would fix their mess when it was they who had to take the first step themselves. In fact, after travelling to over 300 different communities in four years I began to reflect how many communities weren't just not helping themselves, but were actually making choices that were sabotaging their own success, and all the while expecting that success would somehow be brought to them by me. That's when the epiphany struck me.

I would on occasion speak to high school students about becoming successful in life, and though these were usually good discussions, I often felt like I didn't inspire them to do one single thing different with their lives. I felt as though they walked out with some new ideas, but quickly reverted back to the same modus operandi they had been using during all their previous years. If they weren't going to change their behaviour, if it didn't cause them to re-evaluate anything they had done or were going to do, perhaps the entire presentation and discussion was an exercise in futility. So I changed my entire approach to the discussion with them.

I started to ask the students to name ways to ensure that they would *fail* in life. It would take a little time and patience, but after a bit of encouragement and explanation they would understand what I was seeking and we would be on a roll. They would start listing potential causes and I would write them on the board. The top three ways to ruin their lives would usually be things like, "I'd become a drug addict," "I'd get pregnant or get someone pregnant before I was ready," and "I would fail out of school," and that was often enough to get us going.

At this point, I would remind them to pretend their goal in life was to fail in one of the many ways listed, and I would ask them to consider how they would begin in their goal to fail. "For instance," I would say, "if your goal was to become a drug addict, because you want to fail in life and you want to do it that way, how would you start towards that goal today?" After a pause, someone would always put up their hand and say, "Well, if I wanted to become a drug addict and start right away, I would start by smoking a joint this weekend." Invariably a couple of students would turn red because that was what they had done the last weekend.

We would go through the list one by one and figure out what we could do today to be sure to achieve the goal of failing at life. When we would get to the premature pregnancy question I would ask how they could start right now to get to that goal. All of the students would turn red at embarrassment over the impure thoughts they would have, and then we would all laugh. Eventually they would point out that they would have to have unprotected sex in order to achieve the goal of getting pregnant now. Some of the students would suddenly look nervous, because they had been doing exactly that. When we would start to talk about failing out of school, which would mean they couldn't get a good job and take care of their family, they would suggest the best way to start would be to fail one of the tests they had coming up in any one of their classes. At that point they all started to look a little nervous as though they had a sudden inclination to study more, immediately.

The point to the exercise is that everyone has goals and dreams. We all have visions and plans for what our future will entail, and sometimes we even have a roughly drawn road map on how to get there. Almost daily, however, we do things that sabotage those goals and dreams. The connection between what we do today and what we're striving for tomorrow is often not made because it is hard to be eternally conscious of how every single choice we make fits in with our long term plans or where it fits on that roughly hewn road map. Yet, many of those particular daily decisions and choices are exactly those we would make if our goal was to ruin our life.

Those kids that smoked a joint over the weekend weren't trying to become drug addicts. The students having unprotected sex weren't trying to get pregnant or get some deadly STD. The students who weren't studying weren't trying to fail out of school so they would get poor jobs. Yet, in each of those cases, if the goal was to ruin their life, each of those students who made that poor choice had taken the exact first step they needed in order to achieve that goal to perfection. Many of the students walked away from those discussions and came back later to tell me that they completely changed their lives because of it. Students are no exception. Full-grown adults make day-to-day decisions that are equally destructive to the goals and dreams they so eagerly seek.

I came to the realization that what worked to help turn young people's lives around could also work to help turn communities around. Communities all want to be successful and they all have hopes and dreams for their future. Yet, every single one of them makes decisions that may feel right, may seem minor and inconsequential, or may simply suit their short term needs, but which sabotage their long term goals for success. They don't connect how the actions and decisions they make today undermine the vision they have for their community tomorrow. It occurred to me that perhaps the same exercise that changed the students' lives for the better could be performed with the communities that were unwittingly sabotaging their future.

So, on my way back to that community to speak for the third time, I carefully began to write down some of the ways I had seen that communities were ruining their own future with decisions they were making, or not making, day to day. I came up with 13, but you need to know there was no particular reason for that particular number. It simply happened that that was how many I had come up with before I arrived to speak that evening. I have kept the number 13 because it has grown to be the recognizable topic of the speech I first gave that night and have given hundreds of times since. You can very likely think of dozens more and are welcome to do so.

The point to this book and the speech I so often give is not a list of things you actually want to do. The point is that our hopes and dreams are often shattered by actions we do daily that may be causing negative consequences for the future of our communities. It is my hope that this book will help you recognize those activities and actions, but ultimately it is my objective to help you recognize the attitudes that are behind those actions. Our attitudes ultimately drive the choices we make, and it is these attitudes that ultimately lead to our success or our failure as people, as communities, as provinces, as nations, and as a human race.

There is something from the previous paragraph that bears repeating because of its significance. Every single one of the 13 Ways that is outlined within this book is about the attitudes we have that cause our own destruction. The students' action of doing drugs, or having premature sex, or failing school is not nearly as important as the students' realization that they are indirectly choosing failure along with their recognition of the attitude leading to that choice. In most of these instances it is the juvenile attitude to accept instant gratification. For communities the attitudes are often more complex, but the principle remains the same. The ways to kill your community are all based on attitude. More important than gleaning a list of the activities that kill a community is understanding and recognizing the underlying attitudes.

There is a community that appears in this book which I call "Omegatown." Omegatown is not a real community in itself, but a compilation of numerous towns big and small that really do exist, that I actually have come across and that helped inspire 13 Ways. They all have their own strengths and weaknesses, but all were unintentionally killing themselves in one way or another – and in some cases, in multiple ways.

This book is written in the first person because it is based on the "13 Ways to Kill Your Community" speech I have been giving for a few years, but it was co-authored by my friend and colleague Kelly Clemmer. When I decided to run in that very first election it was at Kelly's office that I made one of my first stops. Kelly has been with the Wainwright newspapers since 1999, and at our first meeting in 2002 had been an editor for about a year. He is currently Star News Inc's weekly newspaper Editor-in-Chief.

Kelly helped *The Wainwright Review* earn two awards for best editorial page in its circulation class, in 2006 and 2007; in addition, *The Wainwright Review* and *The Wainwright Star Chronicle* took home number one and two in all of Canada for Best Overall Newspaper within its circulation class, in 2009. I am a good public speaker, but it should be fairly obvious that Kelly is the skilled writer of this duo, and his work on this book as he helped to flesh out the ideas and find the right words to communicate them has been amazing, profound, and appreciated.

Kelly was also involved in this project because he is one of the most community-minded people I have ever met. He chaired the Centennial Celebration Committees for both the Province of Alberta's Centennial in 2005 and the town of Wainwright's Centennial in 2008. He is a founding member of the Wainwright Arts Festival, is the founding chair of the Wainwright Arts Council, and, from 2004 to 2007, was a member-at-large for the Writers Guild of Alberta, including a one-year stint as Vice President. Most recently he was awarded the 2009 Citizen of the Year award by the Wainwright and District Chamber of Commerce. As these awards attest, he has done incredible work in helping to bring arts to his community and for helping its members enhance their quality of life.

We both hope you enjoy *13 Ways to Kill Your Community.*

Chapter 1
Don't Have Quality Water

The first way to ensure that you will kill your community is to neglect the quality or quantity of water. On the basis of my work on rural development, I believe that you could blindfold me, take me into any small community, sit me down at the kitchen table in one of the homes there, and if you placed a glass of water from the tap in front of me, I could tell you almost everything important about that community. When you remove the blindfold, if I see that that glass of water is yellow in colour, has a funny or bad smell, has a bad taste, has a lot of gas in it, or is of poor quality in any other way, then the community will have similar shortcomings. More than likely there will be grungy, dirty streets, boarded up windows on businesses, and old unkempt houses. Essentially the town will look like it is dying.

If that glass of water is clean and clear, however, and if it doesn't have a bad smell, and it tastes good, when I walk out the door of the house, it's a pretty safe bet I'll see new businesses, clean streets, clean windows, new homes, plenty of flowers planted, and in general a town that looks alive. That's because every single person there demands and expects good water.

The simple fact is, people won't tolerate anything less than quality water. You can check this out for yourself. Spend some time in your local gas station. Buy a cup of coffee and sit by the front counter for half an hour and listen to people who come through. You will probably hear every person who comes into that station complain about the price of fuel, but they will not even blink at the purchase of a bottle of water, even though that water is three times the price by volume and is still probably little more than average quality tap water. People simply expect good quality water and they won't settle for less.

Very few people in this world are looking to purchase a house that has yellow water stains running down the tub or around the drain in the sink. Some might accept this sort of blemish in a very old building, but few people purchasing a new house would accept serious staining, given all the implications, real or imagined, that come with it. The natural inclination on the purchaser's part would be to wonder about the longevity of the appliances, and even more worrisome, to wonder about the soundness of the more structural components of the house, such as the hot water heater and the plumbing. The water may cause only the yellow stains and nothing more, but the majority of people aren't interested in finding out. They won't tolerate the problem regardless, which means they won't buy the house – and they might just decide not to live in the community, period.

There are issues with quality of water that run much deeper than merely cosmetic, however. In Omegatown a discussion about the town's water had raged for almost two decades. The town was actually famous for its poor quality water. The sodium and gaseous content of the water were very high, and it sometimes had a repugnant odour. The occasional odour and the high gas content were mostly cosmetic issues that turned people off, but the sodium content became a perceived health problem. The level was well within all the health and water quality guidelines, but everyone still felt uneasy about it. The town became famous for all the wrong reasons, as I realized myself when I heard one person suggest, "If you have a heart condition and want to die, move to Omegatown. If you don't have a heart condition and would like to get one, Omegatown is the place to be."

Not a very nice reputation to have, indeed. Whether problems with water quality are substantive or imaginary, serious or cosmetic, if rumours are being spread that water quality is sub-standard, that perception will take root. Inevitably, an understanding will form that your town is not a good place to work, live, and raise a family. And if that happens, then no one will move there, and if no one moves there, your town will die.

Even though it's important to not have quality water if you want to promote your town's failure, not having *enough* water can ensure failure absolutely. The issue over the quality of your water is a moot point if you don't have enough water to begin with. We can survive for three minutes (approximately) without air, three days without water, and three weeks without food. And if these elements are critical in our lives, then they are also essential in our communities. If we have water we can boil it and filter it to make it potable. If we have no water we are going to die.

We certainly should not postpone dealing with the issue until the amount of water available to us becomes a dramatic life-or-death crisis, however — we should face the problem much sooner and in much less threatening circumstances than this. We all know how the quantity of water is important to economics, long before it ever becomes a serious issue. Competing demands between towns and cities, between states and provinces, and between nations are on the rise. Soon competing interests between those who produce food, those who produce energy, and those who produce goods will occupy much of our discussions about water and its use.

Scarcely a business can exist without appropriate quantities of water. Every farmer will tell you that if they can get six inches of water applied at the right times of the year, given the soil conditions and appropriate climate, they can grow you just about any crop and it will be a bumper one. But we don't control water like that. You can have great conditions, but if you don't get rain it won't grow. If it rains too much beforehand, you can't get that crop planted; if it rains too little, it won't germinate until too late in the growing season. Water is critical if you want to ensure successful primary agricultural production.

Quantity of water is just as critical to the development of value-added manufacturing, and to most tourism development, and it's especially critical in determining the size to which your community can grow. There are communities all over North America that cannot expand because they cannot supply fresh quality water to the new developments' new homes. People, communities, business, and industry need water to grow.

Virtually every settlement around the globe was and is founded in close proximity to water. But in many cases those resources are becoming "taxed or maxed." I do not mean that the water now has a tax on it, though this may happen someday. What I mean is that traditional water sources around North America are starting either to fall under serious strain (taxed) or they are utilized to their full potential now and can't give another drop (maxed). This situation makes for urgent quantity of water concerns that our communities must address sooner rather than later.

The traditional remedy to the quantity and the quality issue has been to build regional water systems in varying sizes to manage usage and quality. Many communities are joining proposed regional systems, and many more are actively working to coordinate with their community neighbours. Such regional water systems can help secure access to large quantities of quality water, and also ensure that the water is used efficiently because of the economic cost-value price that is placed on the water and on access to it. Such secured access can help ensure a community's long term success and viability. However, since our purpose here is finding ways to *kill* the community rather than ensure its success, we certainly don't want to do this.

In Omegatown the residents strove very hard to ensure the failure of their community by fighting any and all attempts to secure good quality and an adequate quantity of water for the indefinite future. Over 15 years ago, the community started discussing what should be done to improve the quality of water. Some wanted to tie into a regional water pipeline system; some wanted a new water treatment plant of their own; others wanted nothing done at all.

The discussion evolved into a vigorous two-sided debate. One side wanted to do something, and the other side wanted to do nothing. Eventually the naysayers lost, and the community bought into the regional water system. For 15 years, however, the naysayers had successfully invented arguments and had thrown up road blocks that prevented any solution from being implemented.

Some argued that it would be too expensive for families to pay, even though the majority of people would still be spending more of their pay cheques on satellite or cable television every month than on the water they consumed. The seniors in the community argued that they didn't see the necessity since the water had been good enough for them when they were younger, or that the pipeline shouldn't go ahead since they themselves might not be around to see the full benefits or returns on a municipal and personal investment being made in the present day. Interestingly, many argued in favour of doing nothing because, they admitted, they either didn't know the facts or didn't want to argue with those who were so passionately opposed to solutions.

Yes, you read that last line correctly. Many people in the community chose not to support the proposed long-term solutions out of ignorance or for fear of the ridicule and arguments they would face from those who did oppose an investment in a solution. Unfortunately, the majority of us behave fearfully in these types of situations. Sometimes it is because we have a tremendous fear of change. Cowardly behaviour not only results from fear, however – it often occurs because fighting and arguing and debating and pursuing take a large amount of personal effort, determination, and concentration, all of which we are often very reluctant to spare from our already busy lives.

These days it seems almost impossible to keep up to date and well informed on all critical issues, so when faced with the question of change it is always easier and less stressful to side with those who speak, frequently with anger and rage, against the change. Doing so often saves us the time and energy of learning the issue, saves us the time and energy of joining in the debate, and saves us the resulting time and energy required to adapt if the proposed change is accepted. As a result, many people prefer just to side with the status quo. The result is that the NIMBYs (Not In My Back Yard), the NOPEs (Not On Planet Earth) and the CAVEs (Citizens Against Virtually Everything) have the usually vocal, angry members *and* numbers on their side.

A rule of thumb I have is that on a petition presented to me, for every 30 signatories there will be one real person with true awareness and concern for the issue. In an email writing campaign I calculate that 20 identical form letter emails are equivalent to one real, informed person who cares deeply for the issue. I measure five form letters (as opposed to individually written ones) mailed to my office as equivalent to one such real person. One phone call to my office, however, from a real person (not associated with a lobby) counted for 20 real people concerned about the issue. One personal letter written to me from a constituent (not associated with a lobby group) was the measure of 30 real people with deep concern for the issue.

The reason for giving personal calls or letters such serious attention is that they usually mean that many other persons are feeling the same way, but have not yet chosen to call or write to me about their viewpoints. After careful research, however, I found that countless petitions were signed by people who often didn't know what they were signing or at least didn't really understand the issue that the petition was about. Countless form emails and letters were signed and sent without the signatories even reading the email or knowing what it was about. It is often so easy, for so many reasons, to join the "anti-change" team who are angry, focused, and opposed to something that they don't have the time to investigate what they are agreeing to.

Yet, petitions continue to have a profound impact on many elected people, and continue to draw signatures from persons who even sign simply because "I saw everyone else signing and they said it was important." I receive few petitions now, perhaps because my position on them is well known. I did, years ago, receive one that claimed to have thousands of signatures and expressed opposition to a regional water project because of the adverse costs it would impose on local people who would be forced to use water meters, which would mean they would have to pay for their water based on use. With perhaps too little political grace I tossed it back immediately and asked them to consider finding someone else to present such an embarrassing declaration of opposition and asked them to consider the following information: water covers more than 70 per cent of the Earth's surface, so it seems abundant to us at first consideration; however, less than 2.5 per cent of the world's water is fresh water. The rest is saline and brackish and therefore not readily available or useful to us for most purposes.

Even more alarming, however, is that less than one per cent of the world's water is fresh, and accessible. Yes, that means that of all the fresh water that exists in the world, which is only 2.5 per cent of the world's water, only 40 per cent of that is even accessible to us. One more time: of all the water in the world the only stuff we can get to and that is drinkable amounts to one per cent of the total. That makes me rather ashamed that we in North America flush so much of it down the toilet.

Now, combine that with the fact that the poorest 20 per cent of the world's population spends more than 10 per cent of their income on water. The majority of us spend more on television than we do on water, and we often cry foul and misdeed if we have to spend two per cent of our income on something we simply cannot survive without. Fully one-sixth of the world's people do not have access to clean drinking (potable) water. That's well over one billion people who don't have access to water as clean as what we flush down our toilets or let run as we brush our teeth. None of us can take our water quality for granted. The World Health Organization says that at any one time half the world's population has one of the six diseases that are caused by drinking poor quality water.

I fully believe that the next great war will be fought over oil, but the last great war of humankind will be fought over water. If you look at it this way, how can anyone possibly say that the cost of water is too much?

Every single one of the 13 Ways that are outlined in this book is about the attitudes we have that lead to failure. This chapter on water, more than the others, may seem to be about infrastructure rather than about attitudes. Though it is an infrastructure issue, I remind you about the attitudes that kept Omegatown from developing a safe and secure quality water supply for so many years. It wasn't really about cost, as most people are willing to pay more money for a frivolity such as television than they are for a life-essential such as water. It was about "why me?" It was about "why does the cost have to fall to me, why do I have to pay, why must I invest?" In other words, the attitudes were entirely selfish, with a result that was often counter to long-term visions of community growth, where it's not about "me" and it's not about "now."

So, you could work on your community members and various levels of government to develop a long term plan for growth in the quality and quantity of your community's water supply. This will help ensure your community's future, because you recognize that people don't demand quality and quantity of water – they simply take it for granted.

However, assuming that your goal is to *kill* your community, then you must ensure there are no plans in place nor efforts made to build on the quality and quantity of the water that your community has access to. Work hard to oppose every initiative, every discussion, and every idea about improving the quality or quantity of water. Start a petition, send form letters, start rumours, imply false motives and conspiracies, exaggerate the costs, or do any combination of the above to ensure that no action is taken, no discussion aroused on the issue, and that nothing happens to improve the quality or quantity of water in your town.

If you do so, every living, breathing soul who has the slightest concern about the quality of water they or their family members drink and every business or industry that must have some security of water supply will leave your community. In time, word will spread and no person, family or business will want to live, work or do business there. In time, your community will shrink much faster than its water supply, and it will die a slow, painful death as though caused by some water-born illness. You will have succeeded in killing your community.

Chapter 2
Don't Attract Business

The second way to make sure that your community is destined for failure is to ensure that you don't attract new businesses. Enticing measures could include competitive business tax rates, appropriate business services, reduced rules and regulations, and a community environment that is friendly to business enterprises. In a small community, however, ensuring failure does not mean simply that you don't attract businesses to your community – it *especially* means making sure you don't attract businesses that will compete with current businesses owned by you or your friends.

Travelling to so many communities over the years has afforded me the perfect opportunity to ask a lot of questions and collect information and anecdotal data on community performance in various sectors and over a range of issues. It seemed rather prevalent that a large number of communities *wanted* businesses and industries, but very few knew how to actually attract them. Some had gone out of their way to hire economic development officers, or put an Open for Business sign at the outskirts of town, and still others had even identified a list of businesses they would like to have, but few seemed to know how or where to start with the process.

I have always found it best to go to the experts when seeking the answer to complex questions, and often the experts are those who have asked and answered the questions already. Those who have set up and operated a business within your community know the challenges to operating there. They will know how taxes affect their chances of success, will tell you what types of business services are missing or poorly developed, and, in general, will have firsthand experience of the business environment.

Of course, if you want to kill your community you can simply disregard that information and those points of view as motivated purely by greed on the part of business owners out to fill their own pockets and get ever more profit and money. Since your goal is to ensure failure, just lump all the good information in with the badly biased stuff and throw it all out, along with the baby and the bathwater. That will go a long way to developing an anti-business environment that will not only make your current business owners feel unwelcome, but will also help ensure that potential new business owners, both local and foreign, would never consider making your community their investment of choice.

There will also be residents who have a firsthand account of what types of businesses and services they would like to see added to the community. They know what businesses are available since they probably utilize them, and they know what is lacking since they have to travel from home in order to get those services. Of course, what people think they want and what they truly need are often two completely different things. A very good place to start would be to take a simple survey of the goods and services that people leave town to purchase, and compile that into a list of the most common needs that are available only outside the community. This will often give you a clear sense of what people truly need within your community, rather than a simple run-down list of what they want. This is beneficial for your growth because often the business that is based on what people need is a lot more successful than one based on what people want.

One of the challenges to a community's success, as I have said before, is its inability to recognize – or perhaps it's a fear of realizing – that its success rests entirely within itself. Sometimes those communities get no further than developing a list of very simple and basic services that are needed, followed by putting up signage inviting out-of-town businessmen to investigate opportunities, or writing letters to corporate head offices asking them to "come on down," or simply waiting for someone to come along and open the business after running some advertisement in some far-off paper.

I wish communities would take that highway sign facing incoming traffic and turn it around so that it faces locals instead, and have it read, "Hey, where are you going? Did you know we are open for business? If we don't have what you are looking for here, did you consider that there may be an exciting business opportunity since 20 other people left this morning to drive to that other town to get/do the same thing as you are doing right now? And guess what, we have 10 business owners who could also use that service who have pooled some money and have a low-interest loan available to you so that we can get you started and grow our community in the process!" OK, maybe that is a really big sign, but you get the point. With a little bit of information on what people leave town for, there may be some local resident who just needs a little push to open that business or provide that service.

A few communities I came across had in fact provided the model of success in this regard. In one example, several of the local businesses and farmers got together – and, more importantly, put some money together – to build a veterinary clinic, something that was needed but at that time didn't exist in the community. At the same time they found a veterinarian who was just graduating and who welcomed the opportunity to take on a new business with a low-interest loan in a community that wanted him to be there. What better opportunity is there than that? The local business owners pooled their money because they realized that farmers who had to leave town to go see a veterinarian in another community also stopped at the hardware store, the feed supply store and sometimes the grocery store, and so on, to pick up supplies as they waited while they were there. All the businesses in town suffered for that, and they knew two things: the problem had to be fixed and *they* had to fix it.

Members of another community collectively bought some housing properties located between a trade college and a university, and signed contracts for free accommodations with regional or local students who met the trade and professional needs of the community and who promised to return to the community to work there once they finished their education. The civic leaders then reported to me that, thanks to their free accommodation plan, the community had overcome a long-standing skilled labour shortfall, and was now partnering with existing tradesmen and professionals to attract new apprentices and business partners to the community. Welders, carpenters, pipe fitters, dental hygienists, nurse's aids, opticians, plumbers, and even their town manager came from this investment. The town leaders indicated they have had a couple of issues along the way but the benefits have far outweighed any perceived or real costs incurred.

So far we have only discussed the issue of attracting new businesses, or rather, not attracting them, in order to ensure the failure of your community. We have not spent much time discussing what to do with existing businesses you already have. It is obvious if you want to drive out your existing businesses to kill your community that you have to ensure they, as well as new businesses, don't have a competitive tax model, that they are encumbered by rules and regulations that make their function costly and burdensome, that they don't get the services they require to operate and that the environment is very anti-business.

There is something that is even more important, however, if you are going to drive out business as part of your campaign to ensure failure. This is going to sound completely ridiculous and counter-intuitive, so I will say it twice. To drive business out of business you must ensure that they have no competition within the community. Got that? Yes, you must ensure that businesses within your community have a monopoly, an exclusive jurisdiction, and that competition is not allowed in.

As I mentioned, all the travelling I've done to rural communities allowed me the chance to ask a lot of questions, collect a lot of information, and make a lot of observations. One of the most interesting of these was about grocery stores in small communities with populations of between 800 and 1,200 people. I found many communities of that size that had one grocery store, and I found almost as many communities of the same size with two grocery stores. I wondered if there was some critical tipping point at which the population suddenly made two grocery stores viable rather than just one.

I began conducting informal interviews with grocery store owners to see if I could determine that population level above which two grocery stores were suddenly sustainable and below which only one could make a living. My research was very informal but I was still astonished to discover that there was no correlation between community population and the viability of the grocery stores in the community. I expanded my search to both smaller and larger towns, with populations of 600 to 1,500 or more people. Again, I saw little correlation at those population levels between the overall success of a grocery store and the population of the community. What I did learn totally astonished me.

I found many grocery store owners who could barely make a living and it didn't seem to matter if they were in a community that had 600 people, or a community of 1,500. Yet, in other communities I could find grocery store owners who claimed to be doing very well, often in communities of 1,500, but also in communities that had fewer than 800 people. Most offered to show me proof of their financial situation and some I took up on the offer, but all seemed genuinely sincere. I had plenty of examples of two grocery store owners in a town of 800 who were successful, but other communities of 1,500 or more that had one grocery story were not. "How could this be? Where was the correlation?" I wondered, and then it struck me. Competition!

I know it must seem counter-intuitive on a grand scale. For a thought experiment let us use two towns of 1,000 people each, one having one grocery store and the other having two. Our business intuition says that the store owner with exclusive jurisdiction over the 1,000 potential customers would have to be more successful than the two grocery store owners who are forced to share the market of 1,000 residents. Our business intuition, however, fails to consider the full value of competition and the fact that these communities are not confined trading areas.

We all see, know, and preach the value of competition. We know competition is good for the economy because it advances the four desirable public attributes: price, quality, selection and service. Competition helps keep the price of goods and services low; it helps ensure that quality is good, and constantly improving; it ensures a diversity of selection and choice; and it prompts better service. We have all learned and witnessed that one of the failures of communist Russia was the poor price, quality, selection, and service of everything from housing to cars to soup, because the absence of competition meant there was no incentive for making improvements in any of those four areas.

Competition is not always about price, but often about, or at least *also* about, the quality, selection (variety), and servicing of the goods and services we purchase. Mottos and slogans about how businesses have the best service, or the most choice and variety, or the quality you can trust abound everywhere. Indeed, some companies have been incredibly successful linking their brand name to one of the above selling points. Everyone "knows" Maytag is a quality product that doesn't break down or else that repair guy wouldn't be so bored. We all feel our uniqueness celebrated when we contemplate the extensive variety of models, colours, shapes, and memory sizes of iPod that are available, and then choose the exact model that is perfect for us. Once we have bought into one of those other competition drivers, the price point is often much less an issue.

Returning to our grocery store thought experiment, we discover that the single grocery store in a community, regardless of its size, has little overt competition to drive its business model – if it even uses a business model. Come now, why would you need a business model when you are the only game in town? Mark everything up as high as you want, because there is no one else in town to buy the product from, right? And why focus on service issues? Service with a smile. Who cares if we smile since no one could shop here more often than they already do. We are the only game in town, remember? Quality and variety? Hey, you get what I get when I bring it in, and until then we have what we have.

The other community, the one with two grocery stores and the same or smaller population, however, has competition. This means they must compete, not only on price, but on quality, selection and service as well. It is a fact of life that no single person can be all things to all people, and the same is true of business. Every successful business finds that they specialize in something that others fail at. People in many communities would say, "I buy my meat and fruit over there because they have the best prices and the freshest product, but I go over to the other place for all of my canned and boxed stuff because you just can't beat their prices and selection." Ah, the sweet sound of competition at work.

So in the community with two grocery stores, people felt as though they got better prices, quality, selection and service, all courtesy of a little local competition. The two grocery store owners shared the 1,000 members of the community, and shared their spending habits as well. In the same-size community with one grocery store, with no competition, and thus with no incentive to offer good prices, quality, selection, and service, residents simply threw up their hands and went out of town to shop. Instead of that grocery store owner having exclusive domain over 1,000 clients, they would usually have less than 50 per cent of the community members as customers, who would buy little more than emergency provisions to last them until they could return to another, often larger, community to shop. That is why the single grocery store would consistently do so poorly.

It's not the lone grocery store owner's fault, necessarily. There is no competition to provide incentives for better behaviour. Of course the owner would always tell me that he or she, and their family, could barely make a living in the town so there was absolutely no need for another competing grocery store in the community. At first blush it would definitely appear that way. In reality, however, though we all understand the value of competition, though we all praise the benefits of competition, though we all welcome competition, that belief often stops the moment we are the ones who are being competed against.

In our composite community of Omegatown there was an entrepreneur who wanted to open a franchise gas station because he thought it would be a good business for the town, and for himself as the owner. Excited, the young entrepreneur went to the town administration seeking to buy land and have it zoned appropriately, to apply for the development permits and building permits, and arrange for contractors as quickly as possible. He wanted to set up a nice late-night fuelling station with a good-sized convenience store, something he felt the town could use, that would help draw traffic off the highway and into town. He had no idea there would be so much trouble to get everything lined up, but alas, he ran into roadblock after roadblock.

After more than six months of getting nowhere, and not having his calls to the town even returned anymore, he gave up. He moved an hour down the highway to another community and had his land bought and zoned and the business up and running in less than a year. When he conveyed that story to me I went back to the original town where he had been rejected and asked around to see what the problem was. Although he thought the town was simply anti-business, it turns out that most everyone in town knew why he had such little luck and cooperation in his attempt to put a gas station within the community of Omegatown. It seems the mayor of the day owned a competing gas station right across the road from where the young man wanted to build his, and the mayor didn't want the competition.

I find it particularly interesting that so many Omegatown residents said they didn't buy gas in the community because the mayor's gas station was the only one in town, and he charged an exorbitant price thanks to his virtual monopoly. The extra high price for gasoline was commonly referred to as the "mayor's gas tax," not because it was a tax imposed by council, but because it was a premium imposed by the mayor who used his position to keep out any competition. Many people would drive twenty or thirty minutes away to buy gas – and then plan their shopping around this purchase – to avoid paying the mayor's gas tax.

Three years later in Omegatown (in this case it actually was the same town as the example above) at least one thing had changed: now there was a new mayor. The real problem remained, however, as another entrepreneur discovered when he tried to open an auto parts specialist store. The entrepreneur went to the town administration to apply for a building permit, and tried to buy the appropriate land and get the zoning approved for the new business venture. It was going to be a great thing for the community. Again, roadblock after roadblock after roadblock seemed to appear, until finally the entrepreneur took the business to a neighbouring community only thirty minutes away and set up shop, again in less than a year. After a little research and a few questions it was revealed that the new mayor was the manager of a competing auto parts store and didn't want the competition.

I found it very interesting that this would happen in the same community so often, so I did some more investigating and found out a lot of interesting things about this particular town. I felt I should call in a man of the cloth as confessional seemed to be the order of the day when the community's secretary told me that a series of welders had been seeking to open shops and buy industrial land there for years. She confessed that she had used her position as the first point of contact within the town office to do everything in her power to encourage them to go away. She would say there was no business for welders around the area, that there was no more industrial land for sale or that it was contaminated, or that the water was bad, or that taxes were too high, and so on. Why? Her husband was a welder and they didn't want the competition.

That's a true story of one community that had three different businesses that wanted to set up shop but were chased away because of the worry over competition. There are thousands of examples of incidents like that in rural communities across North America and indeed your community probably has some stories of its own, whether you know about them or not.

It's an accepted economic principle that each dollar entering your community changes hands seven times. This means that a dollar spent in your community will be spent six more times before it leaves your community. However, a dollar spent outside your community is gone for good, without being spent those six more times. It is obvious that the economic stability of your community depends on those dollars. Without competition to provide incentives for the best price, quality, selection and service, there is less and less likelihood that money is going to be spent at home, which means, as a business owner, your share of the pie grows smaller and smaller.

If killing your community is your goal, then you have got to ensure that new businesses are not attracted. You must work hard to ensure you do not have competitive business tax rates, appropriate business services, freedom from excessive rules and regulations, or an environment that is friendly to business enterprises. It is not enough, however, that you simply fail to attract new business – you must pro-actively drive away all potential new businesses that on their own initiative have shown an interest in your community. This applies especially to any enterprise that will compete with your current business. That way your businesses can fail slowly as consumers and entrepreneurs from your community hightail it out of town for much greener pastures.

Chapter 3
Ignore Your Youth

Youth – men and women approximately 35 and younger – are typically the most energetic individuals within your community, and are full of creative, innovative ideas not yet prejudiced by bad experiences and fruitless pursuits. Within youth lies the hope that anything is still possible if we can just dream it, and the energy and passion to pursue those dreams until their realization. If you wish to eliminate any future for your community you must be vigilant in snuffing out those hopes and dreams, that energy and passion, which are naturally bound up in those young visionary packages of youth within your town. You must ensure that young people are not part of your councils, your chambers, your volunteer organizations, or any committee where that energy or those ideas might find life. It is of critical importance, if you are going to kill your community, that you ensure those youth do not become engaged and active participants in community life. If you are skilful, their energy and ideas will die and your town can be killed. If you are *really* skilful, they will leave town, taking all that energy and all those ideas with them, and there will never be the risk that the hope they embody might rise from the grave to spoil your plans for certain failure.

One excellent measure is to make sure you don't give any thought to succession planning. There are tax experts who travel through rural areas all across North America to preach about the need for succession planning, and for a relatively small sum they will help you do just that. Regardless of where you farm, if you don't appropriately plan for succession you not only risk giving a significant portion of the farm to the government by way of taxes, you also risk leaving very little of the actual farm to your children so that they may carry on with farming after your retirement. As a result, succession planning is not only important to the couple that wishes to retire from farming, or to the next generation that wishes to step in and take over the farm, but is equally critical to the integrity and future of the entire agriculture-based communities. Yet, as true as that may be, I have found very few communities that are planning for succession for town or county councils or other leadership positions – that is, a plan to recruit new community leaders to succeed the older members who are approaching retirement. I originally believed this merely to be an oversight or lack of understanding, and in many cases that was in fact true, but often there was a deeper issue at hand. In some instances I actually heard people express their deliberate desire to keep young people out of local planning and governance. I am not suggesting that all community councillors share this sentiment, but I admit I was astonished to find anyone who truly thought this, let alone someone who would openly admit it. I also discovered that, though only a few were willing to express such an attitude out loud, many demonstrated that belief through practice and behaviour.

I have spoken to hundreds of communities at their request about the need for succession planning within municipal governments. I was shocked the first time I actually had a councillor come up to me after I had finished speaking and, looking me squarely in the face, say that those young people don't know "squat" and they could wait until they were over 40 when it would be their turn. My reaction was to laugh out loud, as I was sure his comments were in jest. I was wrong – he was completely serious. I have heard a few others express similar comments since then, but I was convinced it was a very rare opinion shared by short-sighted old fools who never seemed to have time, patience, or a care for anyone fifteen years their junior. Yet, even amidst expressions of appreciation for the youth that served the community, I witnessed those same people seize every opportunity to attack, embarrass, or demean young persons who dared to speak.

Usually the comments were not, as one would expect, part of a vigorous debate over issues that would affect the future viability of the community, or other such issues that could ignite passions, but often came through in innocuous discussions of relatively trivial matters. It became apparent there was a noticeable (though sometimes unconscious) hostility towards those youth. Overtly there seemed to be a full understanding of the need to educate, engage, and develop those young people into leaders, but deep within many people and organizations I recognized a resentment of the opportunities available to that next generation, and of their influence and success. It was horrendously sad to watch.

I have yet to come across any community except one that does any succession planning for main street businesses. It is so easy to leave succession planning to your businesses themselves to figure out, but if you are concerned about your community's future then the state of your community's businesses, and their succession plans, must be a concern as well. We fret incessantly about the future of agriculture when we recall that the average age of farmers is over fifty-five, but in many of our small communities the average age of business owners is not much lower. Few of these persons are planning for someone to take over their business, and even fewer of those have any understanding that their best options for transition to a new generation of business owners are sitting right there in the community.

Along with many others, when I was in high school I participated in a course of study called Work Experience. It's a program that partnered businesses with high school students to give the students an academic credit for working and at the same time give them a chance to learn about that business from the owner. My work experience was especially beneficial as I laboured throughout the entire program at sweeping floors. Yes, if I am ever looking for a new career or job opportunity I can always fall back on the skill I developed over all those months of sweeping the floor. At the end of the program I found out the majority of my classmates were acquiring much the same experience base as me. Unfortunately that meant that we all might find ourselves competing for the same position in the same warehouse one day.

I don't blame anyone for the manner in which the program was executed. It was simply that the program lost sight of, or never fully developed into, its full potential. There were lots of opportunities for business owners who were starting to think about their retirement and thinking of turning the equity in their business into more time on the golf course. There were a lot of young people passing through high school, wondering what they wanted to be and what they wanted to do with their lives. Many of them had no idea that owning their own business was an option, even though, if they were to learn of that opportunity, they undoubtedly would find tremendous excitement at the prospect. Personally, I was always under the impression that my options were to farm, or to work in the oil patch, or go off to university and perhaps never come back.

No one connected me to the opportunities that lay before me within the community. No one showed me what businesses existed or explained how I could eventually own one. No one showed me what businesses were missing and encouraged me to start one of my own someday. No one explained to me that if I wanted to be a doctor, or a dentist, or a lawyer, or a teacher, or a psychologist, or an engineer ... that I could go away to school for that, and then I could come back. No one did anything like that for me or for the other young people getting ready to graduate. Few communities do that for their youth and for the sake of their own community's future, even though we all know that our communities are continually in need of new businesses, new business owners, doctors, dentists, teachers, psychologists, engineers, and so on.

For the first twenty-one years of my life on this Earth my dad told me I didn't want to be a farmer. He would say to me, or more often I would hear him say to others, that there was no hope or future in farming, that you only get one good crop for every seven years of bad ones and then when you have one good crop, everyone around you also has a good one, so then it's not worth anything. Farming is a lot of work, a lot of investment with little return, little time for vacations or trips, and a lot of thankless hours, as I heard over and over from him and the other farmers in the area. Of course I would hear these conversations more frequently when times were tough, when we had little sleep or when we were having a bad day, which was often enough. I like to point out to my dad, now, that he and our neighbours did a superb job of convincing me that farming was a bad thing to do. Then I like to point out how, when I returned from university with my first degree and he asked me if I was interested in farming, how amazed I was that he actually had the gall to look surprised when I said, "no way."

Within many of our communities we don't just leave our youth with the idea that there are no businesses to build or take over, or that there are no new professionals needed in the community –

we often go to great lengths, deliberate or accidental, to convince them that staying in the community assures them a lifetime of sweeping floors. Our youth become convinced, by our own word and deed, that the future is bleak and the only hope lies outside of town. Just as farmers complain about how awful farming is and then lament that their sons don't want to farm, and that the farmers are getting older, and that no one will be left to grow the food or take over what they worked so hard to build, communities do the same. Communities tell their youth in one way or another that there is no hope in their town, there is no future, and that the youth are not really welcome, and then they lament when the youth really do leave.

I was invited to a particular lunch-hour meeting in Omegatown to advise community leaders how to build a culture of success in the town. We sat down for lunch and I listened to the conversations around the large circle of tables. One gentleman was engaged in a loud discussion about how the community was shrinking in population as fast as it was shrinking in opportunity. He doubted they would bother to keep the hospital open much longer (which was patently untrue and he knew it) and when that happened all the businesses would just pack up and leave. In short, he was a downer and his reasons for being down had more to do with his temperament than the reality of the community.

I noticed as he droned on, however, that the young people around him listened intently as he described the house of falling cards that he imagined was his community. After we finished lunch I did my presentation and then we moved on to questions and answers for the remainder of the lunchtime. I was so enthralled when that negative gentleman was the first to ask a question, but I was even more excited about the question he asked. He said, "Doug, like every other community of our size, our biggest challenge is that youth keep leaving. How do we get our youth to stay here?"

13 Ways to Kill Your Community

Now, as a former teacher I am well known for my patience and decorum in addressing any question, no matter how ridiculous I believe it to be, so I shocked even myself when I simply blurted out, "Shut up!"

I was even more shocked when a round of applause started up sporadically around the tables as people realized why I had said those words. Obviously the gentleman's negativity had been commonplace and they had felt that nothing short of those two simple words could so ceremoniously and succinctly answer his question. I did apologize to the gentleman, who also turned out to be the mayor of the community, and went on to explain to him that telling our youth over and over that there is no hope, and then wondering why they have no future, is a self-fulfilling prophecy and ironic to the core. He agreed and confessed to everyone that often times his leadership role meant he had to listen to complaints and negativity at such a lengthy extent that it consumed him and made him negative against his own better judgement. In the end it was a very good exercise and helped the community purge some very dark demons that people were afraid to fight: namely, that negativity is the prevailing wind that will smash your community against the rocks of failure unless you take the corrective measures to reverse that attitude.

Typically when people ask me how to keep youth in their community I don't tell them to shut up, but I do tell them that the notion that the community is supposed to keep their youth is entirely the wrong one to have. On occasion, when I am asked that question, I even have visions of townsfolk locking the youth in their rooms, or tying them to lampposts on Main Street, or even blowing up roads that head out of town. You shouldn't try to *keep* your youth. The nature of youth is to go explore, to try new things, to seek new adventures. The more they experience of life, or other cultures, or other ways of thinking and doing things, the more well rounded, creative, understanding and thoughtful they will be. This means they will be better community leaders, better business leaders, better social leaders, all replete with broader ideas and concepts that they can exercise within your community.

If your youth are not allowed to explore where adventure lurks, they will never learn anything beyond what they are given at home. This does not mean that all youth have to leave and go exploring, or that there is something wrong with them if they don't, but if they seek to go, you should not fight to hold them down. If you try to keep your youth in your community you risk developing an entire generation that experiences no solutions beyond the town's history and has no vision beyond the town's limits. You risk creating a band of young people who missed the opportunity to witness creativity and adventure and who will almost surely become very small minded and routine.

When it comes to youth, the future of your community is not about finding a way to keep them from leaving, it is dependent on you finding a reason for them to want to come home.

Winkler, a community in Manitoba, is a fascinating case study of youth engagement. Each year, the business and community leaders meet with the grade 11 and 12 students and ask them what they are up to and what they are interested in doing with their futures. The town leaders, both council and business, take it upon themselves to create jobs or business opportunities for the next crop of graduates from the local high school. The community business leaders developed a fund to loan to youth in the community who are interested in starting and building a business but need help getting it off the ground. The town itself invested capital into building a business incubator that helps prospective youth with a business idea and mentorship behind them to start up their business in a place that shares information about best practices and where young people encourage and support each other.

Jobs and business opportunities are created in the community, not to keep the youth who are destined to venture away from doing so, but to assure them that there is a place for them if and when they are ready to return home. They also found an added benefit they had not foreseen: when they created 30 jobs or business opportunities for the 30 youth who were graduating in their community, not all of the youth stayed; but youth from *other* communities, which had not taken it upon themselves to create any jobs or business opportunities, were moving to *their* community. The reputation they developed as a place that was welcoming and encouraging for young entrepreneurial people grew and spread and soon the town was growing quickly, and experiencing a decrease in the average age of their population – counter to what was happening in other communities all across North America. After only one decade Winkler saw their population double in size, and their worries turn from their community's future existence to the community's need for infrastructure. When last I heard, they were successful in maintaining their youth and growing that sector of their population.

The success that this Manitoba community had benefitted from reminded me of some advice I once got from a young woman named Shawna Wallace, who taught me more about engaging young people than anyone else. Shawna was always so dismayed at how nonchalantly people could discuss the dire straits of the youth within their community. She would point out in speeches how she had heard the very people she was speaking to say that, "there were no opportunities for youth in the community," or that "the youth in the community were leaving and would never be back," and how she would watch the very people who said that simply shrug their shoulders and shake their heads as though it was a minor loss. She would tell them to replace the word "youth" in those statements with the word "future," since youth are the future, and see if it was so easy for them to simply shrug their shoulders and ignore their responsibility to do something about it. Go ahead, try it yourself – substitute the words in the statements above and see how it makes you feel. I'll wait.

Pretty powerful, isn't it? Shawna had a couple of other pieces of advice that I found wonderfully effective. She pointed out to me that youth don't believe or take too seriously anyone whom they feel is of the older generation. I thought about that and discovered that if an older person asks a young person to join their organization, say the Elks or Shriners, they simply don't believe they are really wanted. After all, when you see young people at a social gathering, a wedding dance, a fundraising dinner, a pancake breakfast, or just on the street, do you actually stop to talk to them, or sit with them? Not usually. In their minds, the invitation was made either out of a sense of duty but was not sincere; or from desperation because your membership numbers were down and your club or group would fold if you didn't get some new memberships so you had to ask, but again you probably didn't really want them there. Regardless of the reason, you have probably given them little or no evidence that there is meaning or merit to the invitation, so they usually just don't believe you.

In reality, if you want the youth to believe you are serious in your attempts to invite them and engage them in your group activities, as a rule of thumb you have to ask them seven times. You have to ask them if they are interested. You have to ask them again if they are interested, by maybe calling them at home. You have to stop them on the street and talk to them about your group, and about what is happening in their lives if you want them to take you seriously. You need to fill your fundraising table with young couples instead of old friends next time, before you can build up a relationship with them and ask them to consider joining your group. You need to get up from the table full of the usual suspects and sit yourself down with the youth at the next pancake breakfast if you expect them to take you up on your invitation to your next group meeting or function. And don't get discouraged if they don't take you seriously the first time – you have to ask them seven times before they think you mean it. If you don't believe me just ask a parent of a teenager.

Shawna also taught me that there are three levels of youth engagement. It doesn't matter what the organization is, these three levels will invariably apply. The first level of engagement, or more appropriately the lack thereof, is to invite youth in for consultation and to ask them what they recognize as problems and challenges within the community, group, or organization that you are trying to fix. Once the youth have identified those, the usual procedure is that you dismiss them and begin to work on solutions to the problems and challenges they have identified. "Thank you for identifying the challenges, and we assure you we now have our best people working on the solutions." Typically this scenario is orchestrated with the intent of making a group feel as though they have been consulted and listened to, but there is very little real commitment to actually resolve the challenges identified, and though youth may often be inexperienced, they are seldom so naive as to think anything meaningful will come of this type of consultation.

A more meaningful level of engagement occurs when consultation involves a much more active dialogue that results in an identification of the challenges and problems, but also an identification of many potential solutions that could be implemented. Typically this is a very heartfelt and meaningful dialogue that has as its true aim the identification and resolution of challenges within the community or organization. When participants truly seek a solution, this is often the modus operandi, but it still misses one critical element that is always the hardest to implement for people in positions of power to master, that being "letting go."

The third way to engage youth, and frankly any other group, is much like the second level of engagement. You must consult with them on what the problems and challenges for the community or organization are, and to ask them to identify the many potential solutions that could be implemented. After that, however, you cannot simply dispense with them, no matter how sincere your intent to implement the solutions they recommend. To have true legitimacy and to effect the most change possible you have got to engage them in the development of a specific set of solutions that can and will be implemented, and turn power and responsibility over to them to make those changes. It is difficult for those in a position of authority to turn over that power and responsibility, but often to get full and meaningful engagement, to create the leaders of tomorrow that you so desperately need to have today, you must work with youth to give them a chance to take leadership roles, and to learn responsibility.

It is critical, if you are to kill your community, to thwart the power that youth have to effect positive change within your community. They are your future business owners, professionals and trades people who can set down roots, build families and build onto your community. You must hold them down, belittle them and shrink their world so they never challenge your authority or the status quo that you have worked so hard to create. It is essential that any free-minded young thinkers who may desire to explore the world are fully aware that they and their future families and careers are not needed or wanted in the years to come. You must work hard to convince them there is no hope or future in your community for them. If you do this successfully you will ensure there are no youth in your community and with that you will ensure that there is no future for your community either.

Chapter 4
Deceive Yourself About
Your Real Needs or Values

Every single community that exists has strengths and weaknesses. Regardless of its size or the level of services available, from the largest city to the smallest village, every community is lacking in something, in some way, for someone who lives there or would like to live there. It may lack an adequate transportation system, it may have weak community spirit, perhaps it lacks enough day-care spaces, gas stations or grocery stores, or perhaps there are no outstanding activities in the arts. Every single community falls short of perfection or utopian status, and needs something and can find some way to improve itself.

As true as that may be, however, every single community also has something that gives it a competitive advantage over other places down the road and around the world. Each community has something unique and wonderful that it offers its inhabitants or those people wouldn't choose to live there. It may be the great day care available, the fantastic job or career opportunities, the low cost of housing or taxes or services, the abundance of recreational opportunities, or it may simply be a personal attachment that makes it home. Every single community has a competitive advantage that makes people choose it over other places.

When a community assesses its needs, often by doing a SWOT analysis (Strengths, Weaknesses, Opportunities, Threats) or whatever acronym they may come up with next, in effect it identifies what its competitive advantages and weaknesses are. The competitive advantages are not always as easy to identify as you may think. You will likely say, "We live in a beautiful valley, we have the best school system around and we have trees and walking trails. Those are our strengths." You will definitely be able to identify most of them, but sometimes we have blessings right in front of our noses that have been there for so long we forget that they exist. Sometimes it takes a community outsider to recognize some of those hidden, or perhaps more obvious, gems that you should be telling the world about.

Assessing needs or values can help you figure out what to market in your community, what is good about it, what competitive advantages it has to offer over other communities. I am always impressed – negatively – by the failure of communities to market their own strengths and advantages both to their own community members and to the outside world. Preparing a needs or values assessment always has the effect of educating a community about its own strong points, and once this step has been achieved, they are much more likely to get an enthusiastic buy-in that will further strengthen the community, and increase the number of salesmen.

Communities that don't undertake a needs or values assessment, on the other hand, usually have no idea what sets them apart from other communities, what is good about their community that they can sell, and what they can build upon. With no assessment done they have to resort to wonderful clichéd approaches that end up doing more harm than good. I never fail to be amazed by the number of communities that put up huge signs on the highway that literally say "Lots for Sale." I am often tempted to stop in at the town office and ask, "Lots of what?" Seems as though every town has lots of something for sale, but no one ever says what it is.

Yes, I am being facetious. Of course I know they are selling home lots. Everyone knows they are selling home lots. Lots and lots for sale. The thing is, *everyone* has lots for sale. If that is all you have for sale, then there is nothing differentiating you from other communities who also have lots for sale. Those communities have actually *un*differentiated themselves by doing this, and are really saying, "We have vacant lots for sale at a cheaper price than anyone else, and that's all we really have, and our lots are so cheap because no one else wants them because there is really no reason to want to live here." Yup, everyone has lots for sale. When you completely fail to do a needs or values assessment and completely fail to recognize your weaknesses and your strengths, those marketable things that differentiate you from the pack, you will fail perfectly. Success means selling the town, not selling lots. Lots and lots for sale.

Assessing your community's strengths and advantages is critical, but when you assess what your community's weaknesses are, that is often when you find the most opportunity for growth and for change. Recognizing strengths affords you the opportunity to brag about, showcase, and market your community; identifying areas for improvement leads to, well, improvement. I spoke on this topic to one local community and they reported back that they did a needs assessment just as I suggested, with the people I suggested, in the manner I suggested, and they had developed an entire new attitude in the community in just a few short months and, most interestingly, they were running out of things to "fix."

I always recommend that a needs assessment be done by a small group of individuals (no more than twenty, but seven to twelve is best) who are the people of influence, not necessarily the people of power. Apologies to those in power whose egos may be hurt, but such persons are often neck deep in the day-to-day survival of the community and are usually too concerned with issues like budget and staffing. Truth be told, they also are not necessarily the ones who have influence over the public, nor are they necessarily the persons within the community whom the community as a whole follows on issues. Sometimes the persons of power are there simply because of surname, or willingness to serve, sheer will power, or political savvy, but it may not be because of influence. This does not mean that a person of power is not a person of influence, but it is better to focus pursuits on those people who are typically watched and listened to by the majority of the community. They tend to have the greatest capacity to effect change within the community. I will discuss those people more later on in this chapter.

Members of the community I referred to that was running out of things to fix explained to me that the needs assessment meeting with those of influence produced two lists. Copies of the first list, which included the great things about the community that are often understated and overlooked, was posted in the town office and other key places. The second list was of all of the deficiencies that the group of influential people saw within the community. The list was prioritized with the most minor at the top and the most complex at the bottom, and it too was posted in the office. The group of "influencers" was asked to pass the lists around and was encouraged to always sound positive and upbeat about celebrating the good list and fixing the bad one. Word spread quickly.

Within a week a few forty-something men came into the office to see what this list of weaknesses was like. They discovered that the top of the list had just a small painting project on it, and the next Saturday and a few beers later, those men had that easy project completed. The next week saw a few women enter as a group to take on one of the other easy projects. The next week saw two groups come in. Each week, they explained to me, the groups got larger and more diverse, and each week the projects got a little larger, but with more people and some success under the belt, the projects continued to get done. Before long, they explained, items that weren't even on the list began to get done because it seemed that everyone was looking for things to fix.

When a small group of people identifies a small problem that can easily be remedied it will usually *get* remedied – provided it gets identified. Something small that is easily fixed usually builds confidence in those who fixed it, and if they have fun and build a sense of team when they do it, they are more than likely to continue to want to work together on another small project to continue the fun. Of course, success begets success and leads to bigger and bigger groups forming. Everybody likes to be on a bandwagon of success. No one ever wants to be the first one or the last one on the bandwagon but everyone likes to get on when they hear about the fun being had. Of course, bigger and bigger groups naturally take on bigger and bigger projects so that everyone is kept busy and part of the program. Eventually these groups of committed people are willing to take on anything, and as that one community reported to me, before long it starts to feel as though the entire community is engaged and committed.

This leads to success in two ways. First, the community starts to develop a sense of pride and confidence in itself as it has success after success. It starts to develop the attitude that it can accomplish anything that it sets its heart and values on, and once that stage is reached the attitude is self-reinforcing. Secondly, you start getting the reputation outside of town that the people of your community are willing to tackle challenges head on, and there isn't a problem they can't fix. Not only does that reputation reinforce itself as it propagates, but it draws outsiders to your community who want to move there with their spouses, their children and their parents because they want to live in a community that is known for success, because the community's success is their success. New people moving to town means more money spent, more jobs created, more volunteers for clubs, and so on, and so on.

It is easy for communities to make mistakes when doing a needs assessment. I have already discussed how gathering the wrong people is one of the ways to inappropriately do a needs assessment. The biggest mistake is listing the things you assume are lacking in your community as though the goal was to create a perfect storybook town, without ever truly considering what is really needed in the day-to-day lives of the people and businesses and volunteer groups and organizations. Very often we operate on ideas that are in our minds but that don't necessarily correspond with what exists in reality because we over-simplify. It's a tendency to say, "Oh, if we only got a new mayor this town would do much better," but then when a new mayor is elected, there's not a whole lot that changes because in actuality the solution that is needed to bring about the town's success is much more complicated than that.

As a result a lot of communities start off declaring that they need a business plan, and a strategy planning session, and a consultant's report on available opportunities, and an economic development officer, and lots of new commercial and housing lots developed, and a hospital, and a new school, and so on. All this may serve the community well, and it may help with reaching its goals, but often times there are a lot of smaller things that the community needs that can be addressed quickly, cheaply, and without outside help. Perhaps it is as simple as painting the kids' slide in the playground that never gets used anymore. Perhaps it is some after-school recreation activity for youth, or some after-dinner recreation for adults. Perhaps it is a "phone tree" for better communication, or more flowers in the park. There are usually a lot of small and simple items that can be addressed up front that are unique to your community and don't fit into the text book paradigm of needs assessments. Usually the best way to identify what a community's *real* needs are, rather than those *perceived* needs, is for the community to explore what its values are first.

My own thinking on this subject has been greatly influenced by two sources. One of these has been a book called *The Tipping Point: How Little Things Can Make a Big Difference*, by Malcolm Gladwell. Within its pages the author describes how social trends, revolutions, and everything major that changes our culture crosses over a "tipping point" – a specific point when any social trend, revolution or cultural change either tips back and fails, or charges down the hill, becomes a juggernaut and can hardly be stopped. I read that book several times, recognizing the tipping points in my own life, recognizing the tipping points in countless success stories, business ventures and political enterprises.

The book is exceptional at explaining what causes these tipping points, and so it seemed to me that, logically, we should be able to reverse engineering tipping points in a way that would be beneficial to us. Despite that insight, I struggled endlessly for several years to find how to cause a tipping point for community success. I still had it in my mind that perhaps it could be a certain size of population that would ensure success, or it could be revenue levels or a certain amount of cultural or sports activities. Perhaps it was preparing a business plan, or maybe it was some mystical combination of all of the above. I knew there had to be a catalyst that would cause a tipping point, but none of the searching and researching led me to a satisfactory explanation.

That is where the second great influence came into play: an insight that for me was nothing less than an epiphany. The epiphany came during a luncheon discussion with a close personal friend and mentor, Les Brost, one of the wisest and most creative and caring souls I have ever met. Through that lunch with Les I came to understand that mid-life crises are often attributed to a sudden realization that one is getting older, but in reality the problem is much deeper than that. A mid-life crisis is really about a realized disconnect between the life we are leading and the underlying values we tend to ignore. Not every man who goes through a mid-life crisis buys a sports car and gets a much younger girlfriend. That has more basis in shallow Hollywood fiction than in reality. Mid-life crises are more often characterized by a desire to work less, golf more, travel more, and occasionally run off to foreign lands to help poorer people build a better life. It is a simple fact that we all have values that naturally conflict, and we are forced to make choices throughout life. A mid-life crisis is a point at which we push aside our well-served values in exchange for the less-served ones. Regardless of the particular actions, the evidence of a mid-life crisis is in the sudden desire to do things differently and change the course of your life.

Most people enjoy spending more time with their children, and we know the benefits that come from that, but we also recognize the opportunities that come from working hard to make money, such as saving for our children's university degrees. We value both, but we must make a choice of one over the other every day. Often times we get so bogged down in the day-to-day of life that we suddenly look back and realize that some of the values and the corresponding choices dominated our everyday decisions, but others were completely neglected. As a result, when we get older and recognize that our own life is finite, we suddenly realize we neglected to spend enough time with the kids, or didn't spend enough time helping others, or we never took time for ourselves, or we didn't travel to some exotic places we always wanted to go to. Because some of the values we have were completely neglected, we tend to overcompensate due to the shortness of time. Suddenly we find ourselves spending more time with the kids or grandkids, or building houses for the homeless in Guatemala, or buying hot sports cars, or vacationing in Venice.

So much could be avoided – mistakes made, opportunities missed, moments that could have been better appreciated – if we simply took the time to assess our values more often. There will still be conflicts in our values, but one of our challenges these days is not to manage the conflict but to separate what our values *are* from what we perceive our values *should be*. Society says that we should always want to work more hours, that we should always want to get ahead, that we should always want a bigger house, a better car, a bigger TV, and often we buy into those goals without ever stopping to see if we truly value them. It is critical for our own happiness and success that we determine if what we are doing is of real value to us, or if we are simply doing it because the collective mindset has us convinced it is supposed to be a value for us. If we want to be successful as people we have got to push out some of society's implanted values and reinvigorate our own.

That was the moment of epiphany. Success comes from understanding our values. Success comes to communities that understand what they value. It seems so simple and I thought I knew that, but I didn't really get it until that moment. Until the community does a value assessment and honestly looks at what its true values are, it cannot properly identify where it really wants to go.

Omegatown had hired an economic development officer to attract new large businesses, but some individuals in the town favoured preserving the quaintness of the community. They liked the privately owned small businesses and the proven economic benefits from tourists who came for a day or a weekend away from the city for that very reason – the community was quaint, relatively small, and picturesque. This is a not-unusual situation, reflecting an assumption that every community anticipates will help them succeed: prepare a business plan, hire an economic development officer, attract new big businesses … . So in Omegatown they did just that, because they thought that's what they were supposed to do. They did not realize, however, that if their plan were put into effect, they would lose not only their existing – and proven – economic model of success, but also the very nature of the community they valued. So they proceeded down that road, because that's what they thought success looked like… and they never stopped to see that they already were successful, and they already had what they valued. This dispute has been simmering now for years, the two warring factions are still no closer to agreement, and no solution to the problem is in sight.

Sometimes what people *think and say* they value is not necessarily what they truly *do* value. More often, just as with individual people, a community's values are more accurately reflected in its actions than in its words. For example, a community may say that it values being small and friendly, but the actions of the people living there demonstrate that they actually don't welcome outsiders. Their values are not being friendly after all. That doesn't make them wrong. The point is that success won't come to a community deceiving itself about who they really are any more than success comes to persons who deceive themselves for similar reasons.

Another community – which we can dub Omegatown 2 – had a slogan proclaiming they were a town on the move, and that was what they valued. In reality it was only what they *thought* they valued because they were well known for taxing, regulating and criticizing everything and everyone who tried anything new. They illustrated through their actions that being "on the move" was not what they really valued. The tipping point for a community's real success is a fair and honest realization of what their values are.

Everyone needs to find their own definition of success. Once you find out what success means to you, you may discover that you are already there. At least you will find out what you truly value, and then you can set a fresh new course that is designed to hold true to your community's values and your community's needs, rather than its wants and the values society imposes. Ensuring failure means doing just the opposite. Failure means holding on to the typically accepted string of values that measure community success. Failure means measuring your community's growth by fulfilling its wants and assumed needs – for instance, measuring your community's success by the newness of its hall or its arena, or by how pretty the school or hospital are. Failure means ignoring the real situation in your community and following a text book formula for success, ignoring the assets and people and values that your community already possesses.

So, if you want to kill your community, do not identify what your community truly values or what it truly needs and you will never have to satisfy either.

Chapter 5
Shop Elsewhere

I have always pointed out that money and finance are often given too much credence as key factors in finding solutions to our modern problems. On occasion money is part of the solution, but if it is, it is always the last step in a solution that requires much more work to be completed before money even comes into the picture. The temptation, and often what seems to be a quick solution, is to throw money at the problem to make it disappear. That is why you often read headlines such as, "Government announces $20 million to reduce youth crime," or "$28 million added to budget to improve attendance at universities," or "$100 million announced to strengthen rural communities." Watch for them. They are everywhere. Rarely does the money even identify the root of the problem, let alone rectify it. The problem never goes away just because money shows up.

In fact, the exact opposite is often true. While money, or more money, is rarely the solution to solving any problem, and is never the first step in addressing that problem, it *can* be a part of *creating* problems. I am not talking here about the apparent lack of funds that communities have to address the needs of their citizens, but about the individual choices citizens make in how they spend money and the consequences those choices have on their fellow community members. It is critical to remember that a community is simply defined as a group of people with a common interest or pursuit and some shared values. As such, many types of communities, including small towns, survive and thrive without money ever being an issue. In many cases, however, it does become significant, and in some cases extremely so.

Many small communities around the world exist without money for infrastructure, even without money to buy and sell goods to each other. In many cases they do very well and continue to grow because they have not lost sight of what values and beliefs brought them together as a community. In many other communities the foundation has changed from a shared understanding of communal values to a relationship that is strictly based on economic principles of goods and services, supply and demand. As such, the circulation and growth of money within the community is important to the survival and prosperity of the community itself, since that is its foundation. That means a great way to kill many modern communities is to spend your money outside your community or not spend any money at all. Either way will ensure that there is a reduced level of economic activity, and since economic activity has become such a foundation of our communities – a foundation that is built upon business-consumer interactions and transactions – you can weaken and eventually kill your entire community.

Every Chamber of Commerce in every city or town preaches that you must keep your dollars at home. We know the importance of this since, according to economists, every dollar spent will touch six more hands within the community before it leaves. Every dollar spent outside your community, however, is gone for good and we know how negatively that can affect a local economy.

So, Chambers always preach the importance of shopping locally because, quite frankly, we all know that shopping elsewhere is a great way to kill your community.

I appreciate that Chambers of Commerce preach that message, it is important, but there's more than just shopping locally – there's a total mindset that has to be changed If you are a long-time resident of your community you have probably witnessed a very strange phenomenon that I refer to as the three stages of local business failure.

Stage One happens when a new business first opens. What ensues is a lot of very negative conversation in the most negative, falsehood-infested place that ever existed on this continent: the coffee shop. Everyone sits around in the coffee shop and gossips. Rarely is anything positive ever discussed in the coffee shop and frankly, not a whole lot of truth is normally spoken there either. First there is a discussion about why you opened the business. This usually involves comments about how it is a stupid idea, how it will never fly in town, how you can't make money at that business, how the products will be garbage or too expensive, and generally any other excuse that can be mustered to explain why no one should patronize you. That is the essential point of this stage: to ensure people do not patronize the business when it is only in its infancy.

Stage Two occurs when the business has been around for a while and even becomes successful. That is when the coffee shop discussion changes. The discussion now focuses on the wealth that the business owner and family are acquiring, and discusses the size of their house, the size of their rings, the quality of their cars, the newness of their golf clubs and so on. The point of the comments and discussion is to stir up some intense feelings that cause others to want to not shop at that business. As a result, consumers drive down the highway to the next community with a comparable business and make their purchase there. In other words, they are simply going to make the next person down the street wealthier while their dollars leave the neighbourhood or the town for good.

Stage Three is more an expression of my own personal anguish over the experiences of so many telephone calls that have left me momentarily exasperated and defeated. In the third stage the business usually goes broke, or relocates to some nearby location where it is more appreciated, or the owner sells out to a larger chain. Then some of the local coffee shop customers call me and ask what the government is going to do to help keep local business owners successful and in the community. Yes, you read that correctly. I would actually witness community members working hard to ensure no one spent money at local businesses and then when the local businesses finally weren't local anymore, those same people would call me and ask me when the government was going to fix it. They were in effect placing responsibility for remedying the situation they created in someone else's hands. More of that will come in Chapter 13.

This great work that people do in places like the coffee shop is often based on some high-minded moral belief that business owners are making too much money and must be kept in check. In reality it is simply jealousy at work. Jealousy is the most evil of all human traits. It is the most irrational, illogical and destructive because it does not simply harm yourself, but also harms everyone else around you. In some cases, jealousy can reach such a level that the more successful your neighbour is, the larger you want their failure to be. When the discussion at the coffee shop sneers about a new business that is opening, the real reason to run it down is usually not that the business is a poor choice, but rather that there is a deep-seated jealousy or envy towards the person who opened it. As the business succeeds and prospers the comments are not really about keeping the business owners honest, but are rooted in a jealousy over the success and the "things" that success brings. Wishing ill to anyone is almost always rooted in jealousy.

If you are jealous of the success and the wealth that your neighbour business owner has, and you refuse to shop there because of it, and you encourage others not to shop there, in all likelihood the business owner will make less money. If that occurs then that may mean fewer employed people in your community. It may mean fewer donations within your community. It most assuredly will mean less money flowing in and around your community. It may eventually mean that the business owner loses money, has to close up shop, loses the house and the car and the rings and the clubs. There now, didn't that make you feel better about yourself? Now there is nothing to be jealous of because the business owner, their success, and their things are all gone.

But wait – there's more to come. Not only is there the loss of that business, there will also be the loss of the jobs and the people that filled them, the loss of the money spent and donated by the owner and all the employees in and around town, the loss of the tax revenue, all of which will have a ripple effect across the community. It is unlikely that you, your job, your family, your paved streets, your school, your hospital, your town hall, or much of anything else could survive if all your jealous instincts were fulfilled and successful business owners were all led to failure. It is not only the business owner who will have suffered to appease your jealousy, but all of the employees who lost their jobs, the service clubs that were supported by that business, and so on. These will be the casualties of your successful campaign of jealousy. Eventually, such a successful campaign can and will come full circle to hurt you and those close to you. That is why jealousy is so illogical. Embracing it leads to the destruction of the successful person you are jealous of, which may in turn lead to your own destruction.

You will argue that people don't honestly mean others ill when they are jealous, and don't cause harm, so I shouldn't be so hard on them. Please recall that the central purpose of this book is to point out the very real impact our attitudes have on the success or failure of our lives and our communities. These are not fanciful tales, but real-life examples I have experienced first hand of how wrong attitudes destroy our communities. Of course we don't see the effects play out immediately or overtly – if we did we would change our behaviour. It is the long term consequences of unconscious decisions that we must avert if we are looking to ensure the health of our community. Jealousy produces a poor attitude as effectively as any other force, and causes some of the most destructive behaviour possible. Whether it simply means not signing up to volunteer at something because the organizer is so much more popular or smarter than you, or not picking up something you need because you would have to go into "that" store and give "that" owner money, or driving out of town to shop because of that new car the owner parks down the street, the damage is done. It really doesn't matter that it is just a feeling or an attitude. It is destructive. Small efforts compound to have great effect, and there is no such thing as a negative attitude or action, no matter how small, that does not have an effect. Of course, if you really want to kill your community, continue with that attitude. You will be just like that high school student who figures there can't possibly be any harm in smoking one little joint.

It has been quite a while since I ran for my first nomination for the Legislative Assembly, but I clearly remember a discussion with the accountant at a vehicle repair shop in a county that neighboured mine. I was anxious to present my case for why she should support my efforts to win the nomination of the party. I had worked hard to prepare so as she fired question after question at me my confidence grew as I responded with well-thought-out, carefully reasoned answers. At the end, she paused as if to size me up and then asked me one question I had not prepared for at all. She asked me how she could be sure that, if elected, I wouldn't go to the capital and simply fight for my county and leave theirs to fail.

That was a great question. I had neglected to consider the rivalry that had existed between the two municipal districts for longer than I had been alive. The fight for the party nomination had often grown to be a fight between municipalities, with the one with the larger population base usually winning. Since I hadn't prepared for that particular question, I knew an answer from the heart was the best. I guess my explanation must have been persuasive, because not only did she agree to support my candidacy, she became an active campaigner on our behalf. She clearly recognized the importance of the larger point: that it is not possible for one area of the constituency to be prosperous and successful while other parts did poorly. If one grows, the others have the opportunity to do well with them, and if one does poorly the others will eventually be dragged down as well. Simply put, no one region can truly prosper in isolation. There is no such thing as a win-lose relationship in cases like this. We all win or we all lose.

It is important that Chambers of Commerce are actively teaching and preaching about the benefits of shopping locally. It is unfortunate that no Chamber, to my knowledge, teaches or preaches to its own membership about the importance of giving members of the community a *reason* to shop locally. Whenever we spend money, we usually like to feel that we got the best bang for our buck and that our dollar was well earned by the business we patronized. From Chapter 2, "Don't Attract Business," we learned about the importance of price, quality, selection and service when it comes to attracting people to spend money in your store. It is unfortunate that some business owners have so strongly bought into the belief that you must shop locally that they have all but abandoned the competitive notion that would encourage them to earn your dollar. Instead it seems that they expect you to shop in their store, that it is some sort of moral imperative that requires no support on their side.

Have you ever entered a business and noticed that the quality of customer service was dependent upon the business owner's mood? Perhaps you have noticed that the quality of the service you get is conditional on whether your son or his son won the hockey game last night? Or perhaps it is simply that look you get for coming into the store just then and interrupting that phone call. Regardless of the reason, it is disheartening and discouraging to a customer coming into the store to not feel welcome. This is not a good incentive to entice the customer or client back. I understand that businesses have the right to go out of business by offering poor service, selection, quality and price. That is the nature of the free market. Business owners do not, however, have the right to complain when customers leave town to spend their hard-earned money in a place they feel appreciated, when those very business owners are the reason that the customers are leaving – yet so many of them do just that.

Recall the story from Chapter 2 about the mayor of Omegatown who owned a gas station and managed to chase away everyone who tried to open up competing stations. He charged a lot more for his gasoline than neighbouring communities, and he could because there was no competition, with the result that many people from the community filled up elsewhere whenever they were out of town to avoid paying the "mayor's gas tax." I was the guest speaker at that town's Chamber meeting and that same mayor actually complained that fewer and fewer people seemed to realize the need to shop locally because they were always heading out of town to shop. I was completely lost for words to communicate that his prices alone had many people leaving. He expected them to pay an exorbitantly higher price. He expected them to shop locally. He was essentially saying that he didn't have to give them a reason. When seeking ways to incite someone into action I have always found that simply expecting them to act the way you want them to and then complaining when they don't is not a good motivating factor.

The relationship between the costumer and the shop owner is a little bit like a marriage, or at least it should be. In a marriage, if either, or both, partners take the other for granted it is not long before they start to feel unappreciated and unloved. If community members begin to take their local businesses for granted by not supporting them, the support they get from those businesses may not be around very long. I have an example from my own experience. Another resident of Omegatown was a man whom I thought I knew well and whom I greatly respected for his apparent dedication to his community. Let's call him Bruce. As it turned out, Bruce was the epitome of a man who took his local businesses for granted. Local business owners would donate to all of the groups, committees, and functions that he worked for because he was the most active volunteer in the community. Eventually, however, the donations began to dry up and word spread that if you were trying to sell tickets or raise money you were better off not having Bruce involved in your function or organization. The reason was that Bruce would go into each business and ask for money for the cause, and each time would make some biting comment that he did all his own business in another community. Bruce could never see the irony in asking for funds for community causes from businesses in his community that he didn't support.

Business owners themselves are not necessarily innocent in this relationship either. Often business owners adopt the notion that people have got to shop locally so there is no need to keep the romance alive. They assume there is no need to clean up once in a while, help with the bags, rush to get the door, or smile when the customers enter. Instead, both the business owners and members of the community have to remember not to take each other for granted. I don't want to over-emphasize the marriage comparison, where you remember to buy each other flowers, just cuddle sometimes, and sit and talk, but it is important to show appreciation and understanding to each other in order to grow in a mutually dependent way.

If you want to ensure you kill your community, it is incredibly important that you take each other for granted. It is important that neither the local shops are patronized nor the local community and customers are given a reason to shop locally. As long as that marriage continues to weaken you can encourage the disconnect within your community. There is a natural tendency for strong communities to grow together in a symbiotic relationship, so you may want to invest some time building a culture of jealousy by hanging out at your local coffee shop and spreading falsehoods, bad rumours, and ludicrous statements about each group. With enough effort it should be possible to break down any good relationship. This will encourage dollars to leave town as quickly as possible, which will make every single person in town poorer. It will also increase the unemployment and the availability of donation dollars that would typically be used to support community growth. If you are truly skilled and successful you will find your community has died a quick and painful death that infests its remaining inhabitants with fear, jealousy, and hate. You will find in the end that you can finally let your jealousy go because there will be no one and nothing to be jealous of, as nothing in your community shows any sign of success.

Chapter 6
Don't Paint

You read the chapter title correctly. If you want to ensure that your community fails then you have to make sure you don't paint. Of course, painting isn't the only factor included in this concept – it encompasses anything that may beautify your community such as sweeping, cleaning, planting flowers, mowing grass, picking up garbage and so on. Essentially, if you want to kill your community then do not do anything that would make it look visually appealing.

You are probably muffling a snicker as you consider the superficiality of what I say. After all, what I have just suggested is that we can actually judge a book by its cover, which seems to go against everything we have been taught. In reality, we were told not to judge a book by its cover because what the cover shows is not necessarily indicative of the contents. That is completely true. What is also true is that people most often do judge books by their covers, or publishers would not spend so much time and expense designing them.

People judge most everything by their first impression of the item's outward appearance. It's genetically encoded into our existence. Not just humans but most animals exhibit the same basic self-preserving instinct for first impression assessment of what they see. Without that ability how would animals – or humans – know if something they have seen is dangerous to them, or safe and friendly? Granted, you may be finding it hard to equate an animal's instinctual assessment of the horns and teeth and claws of another animal to the idea of whether your town is beautiful and attractive enough. Our animal instincts go beyond simple assessments for personal safety, however.

All animals are also genetically predisposed to enjoy aesthetically pleasing things. Imagine a female leopard walking around the jungle feeling a little lonely and looking for a mate. Suddenly two male leopards appear on either side of her and each gives her a friendly wink. As she looks them over she notices that one of them has bright eyes, nice clean shiny fur, sharp claws, and otherwise looks attractive, healthy, and strong. The other, though very friendly, has a broken tail, mangy fur, droopy ears, an infected eye, and otherwise looks unhealthy, sickly and weak. Which do you think she will choose as a mate? Sure, we could say she is out for that large gazelle that the healthy one caught, or we could say the she-leopard is superficial and puts too much emphasis on looks, but in reality, she is choosing who will be the best provider and the securest mate as based on appearance. Frankly, I would agree with her.

Many of those behaviour patterns are basic to us, and as much as we believe we have evolved beyond such animal instincts, we are no more advanced than the leopard. How often have you looked across a crowded room, seen a person not physically attractive to you and decided, I'm just going to run over there and ask that person out? Have you or anyone you know of walked into a car dealership and asked to see all the ugly cars? No one meets with a real estate agent to purchase a house and insists that "ugly" be one of the distinguishing features of the home. We all want to be surrounded by beautiful places and things. We are all attracted to aesthetically pleasing people.

I am certain that I could pluck someone from a large urban city, take them blindfolded in a car to the main street in certain rural communities I can think of, and when they pulled off the blindfold they'd be rolling up the windows and locking the doors as they drove from town. To a resident of the community everything might seem fine, perhaps a little run down or dirty, but to those folks from the urban centre the community looks a lot like a neighbourhood that has a high crime rate and is probably dangerous. Their instinctive first impression tells them that it is not a place they want to be. You can lament how unfair it is, but unfortunately it is what it is and complaining about the situation and circumstance won't fix anything. Sure, people can argue that aesthetics are only skin deep, but when it comes to a community, it is not only about the aesthetic appearance, but the feeling people get from the appearance. That negative feeling keeps people from wanting to visit, shop, or live there. Obviously if you are looking to kill your community, don't paint and the poor aesthetics will create poor feelings that will drive people away.

I was explaining some of these concepts to my wife and she suddenly insisted on taking me shopping. Normally I hate shopping, but in the face of her insistence we went to two large and popular department stores. Both department store chains were owned by the same company, although I was not aware of this at the time, and about half of the goods sold in one were also available in the other.

In the first store we went into, the linoleum flooring was curling up in places or had come completely off, leaving only the tracts of dried glue to walk on. The stock on the shelves wasn't stacked neatly and in some places it looked as though a hurricane had blown through. The staff seemed to want to be anywhere but at work, appeared irritated by my presence, and sloughed around in badly fitting and overly worn department store uniforms. I noted the prices on some particular items, which my wife assured me were excellent deals. As we left the store an odour of staleness burned into my mind.

We went directly to the other, fancier store and I instantly noticed the difference. As we walked in, beautiful clean carpets acted as runways between individual garments that were all neatly and orderly hung and easy to access. Everything smelled good, and soft, soothing music played in the background. We weren't there two minutes before an attractive woman approached us and asked if we needed help finding anything. My wife showed me the same products as I had identified and priced in the other store and to my astonishment the prices on those identical products were remarkably higher than in the previous location. I presumed that the fancier store would have trouble moving that portion of its merchandise that could be bought for less in its sister store and would, therefore be in dire financial straits. To my surprise the fancier store was more financially stable and profitable than the other.

Why would anyone go to the fancier store to pay twice or three times as much for the same goods they could buy in the other store? My wife finally had to explain to me that in a society with such affluence many people have the luxury of choosing a pleasant shopping experience over simply shopping for value. As such, many people will choose to shop in a place that is warm and friendly and inviting and, yes, aesthetically pleasing when they have, or can afford, the option. Just as many people, when they can afford it, will choose the fancier vehicle, the bigger house, the better diamond, the popular clothes, they will also pick the fancier store – for the aesthetics.

Now, before anyone decides to write me an email on the evils and horrors of consumerism and capitalism and before calls start coming about how we have too much affluence and are too superficial in our lifestyles, you're talking to the wrong man. Whatever my feelings are concerning the value of the choices consumers make, they're irrelevant. The purpose of this book and my observations is to show the attitudes that drive people's choices and guide their lives and how you can use those attitudes to help your community fail faster. It is worth mentioning that if you truly do want to kill your community it is beneficial to be drawn off focus so that you direct your efforts to fruitless pursuits that have nothing to do with your future success. In other words, if you are reading this book to see how to turn your community's fortunes around and, drawing upon the above commentary, you change your focus to begin a campaign against superficial consumerism, then congratulations, your community is well underway to failure under your guidance.

My wife and I went looking for a house shortly after we were married. As we cruised through listings and living rooms I noted there were specific houses that my wife liked and others that she really didn't, but it was difficult for me to determine exactly what the qualities were that made the difference. A realtor friend identified what I could not and boiled it down to a very catchy phrase they call "curb appeal." If the first impression was favourable – the lawn was nicely manicured, no paint was peeling off the window trim, flowers were planted in the flower beds, and so on – then my wife was initially impressed and opened up to the options and opportunities that the house afforded. However, if the house lacked that curb appeal effect when we pulled up, often it didn't matter as much what the house looked like on the inside. The first impression had narrowed or even closed off the option to consider what the rest of the house had to offer. Real estate agents know how important curb appeal is in addressing that first impression that lingers through a viewing of the house. People are drawn to aesthetically pleasing things, and homes are no different.

I drive over 100,000 kilometres a year and my wife travels with me when she can. When we decided to purchase a new vehicle I asked her to keep her eyes out for what appealed to her and point it out so I could begin to recognize what type of vehicle she would prefer. We knew we needed space for the boys and bags, so trucks and small cars were out, but everything from the mini-van, SUV and cross-over categories was on the table. I thought I had an idea of what she was looking for based on her indications on the highway, but each time we got to the vehicle lot to actually view the vehicle in question, she was usually not particularly fond of the make and model on display. I soon realized that what my wife was doing was identifying vehicles within the class type we sought, but was expressing interest in the vehicles based on the colour, and often, when we viewed the vehicle on the lot in a different colour, it didn't have the same appeal. It was the aesthetics of how the paint looked on that model, not the model itself or how it drove. Those things were important too, but the feeling of the nice colour was more of a factor than I expected.

These observations most certainly do not reflect any superficiality of judgement; my wife is a deep and spiritual person who recognizes not only the value and importance of beauty, but deep, intrinsic quality as well. Whether we are discussing a home, a car, or a building, appearances are important. Communities have found many ways to improve their curb appeal, and enhance that first impression, by utilizing paint alone. I witnessed some communities that painted their fire hydrants to brighten up the corners of town. One community had arranged a regular "paint week." Everyone in the community brought all their older and partial cans of paint to a central location where someone with aesthetic savvy would mix and blend paints with the help of a paint recycling expert into fantastic bright colour schemes. Everyone would then gather on a following weekend to paint some pre-identified old fences, or old buildings, and other fixtures that were bringing down the aesthetic value of the community.

In essence the community coordinated their efforts to beautify their town. Some other communities went a step further and hired a professional painter to paint historic murals on large bare walls that would otherwise be unattractive. There was a significant recognition that paint was a simple way to improve the community they lived in, and the beautification had an inherent value that enhanced the quality of life of the residents, and the community's prospects for future success. I always find it ironic, however, that even in communities that recognize the intrinsic value of good aesthetics, the tax system is often set up to discourage private residents from sprucing up their own private property. Too often when a resident tries to make improvements, even by planting a few trees, the taxes on that property go up. Residents do what they can to enhance their own property and the town, but in the end pay more in taxes because of land improvements and property taxes.

I know of one community that developed tax incentives/ reductions for businesses that invested to beautify their main street business assets. The program was a smashing success, as most every business took advantage of the offer. They painted and built planters and otherwise improved the aesthetic of the street level and front space that greeted customers. Two old abandoned buildings on main street were purchased, renovated and painted, and sold to new businesses under the program. The result was that throughout an entire summer there was an incredible increase in traffic of people from other towns who wanted to see what had been dubbed the prettiest main street in North America. The town administrator confirmed that what was originally lost in forgone taxes was more than made up by taxes that would come in future years from the two new businesses and the rejuvenated businesses that resulted from the program. The town is now considering options for a similar program for residential properties.

Across Canada there is a volunteer organization called "Communities in Bloom" that brings together persons and groups who wish to beautify their cities, towns and villages. The purpose is not just to clean up garbage and plant flowers around the town, but also to leave a lasting encouragement for the people of participating communities to take pride in what they have. The work that these volunteers do through this program is infectious, causing others within the community to tidy up their own yards and do their part to keep the work of the volunteers going.

I've seen many towns and villages, using just a little elbow grease, make their dumpy, dusty, run-down-looking communities appear successful and vibrant. I emphasized that they made their run-down-looking communities *look* successful and vibrant, because in all honesty, appearances can be deceiving. Sometimes our initial first impression can lead us astray, or rather the information we get doesn't really demonstrate the inner workings as we would presume. There is no doubt that can often be the case, and a beautification program by itself may not be enough – but it's usually a terrific start. We have to remember that an ugly appearance will never bring in that butterfly tourist, and will do nothing to build pride among the members of the community.

So, if you want to ensure failure, don't paint. Of course failure will take more than that. It may take a concerted effort to turn your town ugly and of course that will only create the facade of failure, it will only create the illusion that your town is dying, and in essence it will only put an ugly cover on your book. With patience, however, no one will pick up that book to read, no one will be attracted to your community and eventually that illusion of failure will become a reality.

Chapter 7
Don't Cooperate

From our first day in kindergarten we have all been taught the importance of learning how to cooperate with each other. Some of us learn the lesson sooner, and better, than others. Some don't learn the lesson at all, but even if we fail to put into practice what we know, we still understand the importance of the lesson. Almost everything takes cooperation to be successful. It doesn't matter if it is in your business, your marriage, or partnership, or even your sports team, cooperation is required. Unless you just arrived on the planet and have never seen another human being in your life, you have had some point or moment when you have cooperated with others, and have experienced the value that comes with cooperating. Some of you may have experienced cooperation on such a high level that you discovered synergy, which is the effect of accomplishing a higher quality and quantity of work because you act as a group rather than a collection of individuals. Regardless, if you want to ensure the death of your community you must not cooperate with other people, other organizations, or other communities.

There are two things in particular that will help you in your campaign: first, communities, especially smaller ones, are often places where everyone knows virtually everyone else; and second, the volunteer base for taking action to build the community is often limited. It is, therefore, a very effective strategy for those volunteers to refuse to work or cooperate with one another on the enterprise of growing your shared community. You can refuse to cooperate on an individual level, or you can expand that to refusing to allow your group or service club to partner with another group or service club on a shared project of interest. Better still, try your hardest to prevent your entire community from partnering with neighbouring communities, especially if those communities understand how working together assures everyone a greater chance of success than working independently.

The choice to not cooperate, however, is merely a passive method to ensure the failure of your community, and as a result can lack true effectiveness. Refusing to work with another person on a project will simply mean that that person and others will proceed without you. You may feel that the project is doomed to failure without your expertise, brilliance, and magnetic personality but in reality, few of us are as important and critical to a multi-person enterprise as we'd like to believe. Personally, I rarely take a day off for fear that everyone I work with will suddenly realize how well they can still work without me. Joking aside, those others you refuse to work with will proceed down their path regardless of your presence and in all likelihood will succeed.

If your group refuses to work with other groups who have embraced a shared vision on a critical community project, or your community rejects the invitation to work with neighbouring communities who have discovered the value of partnering for success, there is always a chance you will still not cause the collective failure of those others. In reality they will carry on without you and maybe even achieve success. You may suggest that regardless of the other groups' or communities' efforts you can still cause the failure of your own group or community, and that is truly your primary goal, but understand that you and your group and your community are not islands unto themselves. In reality, no matter how much you wish to fail, the success of the groups and communities you refuse to cooperate with could still spill over into your community and consequently, regardless of your own passive refusal to cooperate, you may experience a trickle-down of success.

Fear not, however – there is another, more effective way, to ensure the failure of your group or community. Rather than taking the passive approach of simply refusing to cooperate with others you can take an *active* approach and begin an aggressive campaign to compete with those other groups within your community, or even with other, neighbouring communities if the opportunity presents itself. Competing ensures that groups and communities are directly pitted against each other even when they have the same goals, thereby expending precious resources on the battle rather than on the goal. This method is very simple to follow through on and can ensure not only that your group and community fail but also that failure extends to neighbouring groups and communities. This will safely inoculate your community from the unwanted success of your neighbours, and will ensure that your campaign to bring about its failure is fully effective.

In Omegatown there were four community organizations that had all decided they needed a new community hall. Residents had discussed for some time the need for such a hall and were prepared to support the building of one. So, all four groups set to work. Oh, I should clarify that in this community of 2,000 people, four organizations were each vigorously working to build their own separate hall. This in itself may seem ridiculous, but it gets worse. They had all decided that simply refusing to cooperate in the construction of one hall was not good enough. Instead, each group competed for the same volunteer base, the same community fundraising dollars, the same government grants, even the same lot in town for the building site! Of course, few people wanted to contribute to four separate community halls so they refused to donate their time and energy, or their money. The town wouldn't give the lot to any of the groups because they did not want to be seen as choosing a winner in the competition. The government, faced with four competing grant requests for identical projects in the same community, refused all of them. Two of the groups even decided to have fundraising dinners on the same night in a bid to outdo the other in the fight for the community hall. No one in the community showed up to either dinner and both organizations almost went broke.

For over ten years those four organizations did everything they could to actively compete with each other, and successfully ensured that no community hall was built. In the end the two organizations that tried to have competing fundraising suppers were so devastated by the competition that they had little left in the way of money or volunteers to continue the fight and dropped out, opting to just passively refuse cooperation with the remaining two groups. The remaining two groups carried on for a couple of more years, passively refusing cooperation where they could, actively competing when one made progress over the other, until finally they saw the light and began to cooperate. Within two years of an agreement to work together they had raised most of the money they needed from within the community, had a strong volunteer base and completed construction of the hall. They accomplished in two years of cooperation what almost a decade and a half of competition had managed to prevent: success.

Amazingly enough, only a short distance from Omegatown was another community that seemed equally determined to bring about its own failure. The two communities refused to cooperate and had managed to compete for anything and everything, to the detriment of both, decade after decade after decade. Never had their ability to extend their competition to the point of mutual failure been clearer than when an industrial corporation came to the communities to see about building a new manufacturing plant in the area. The corporation had expressed interest because of the available labour force, the proximity to the rail shipping lines and the lower cost of business there. They expressly asked the two neighbouring communities to jointly work on how they would address the increased need in housing, the growth in the school population and demand for health services, how they would share tax revenue and any other growth pressures that would result from a new manufacturing plant. These were concerns that many municipalities across North America would love to have.

Unfortunately the communities did the opposite. Instead of working together they competed and argued over who would get what share of revenue. They argued about where the plant would be located, where the people would live, where the children would go to school, which hospital should be expanded, and who should get more of the revenue generated. None of those choices were really up to the communities to make, but their competitive instincts lead them to try and grab what they could from the other, hoping that all the success derived from the manufacturing plant would be theirs and theirs alone. The corporation knew that one community could not handle the entire project and the influx of new people so they wanted cooperation. They were disappointed that they didn't get it. So disappointed were they, in fact, that they got up and walked out of a meeting when the community leaders began to argue, and they never came back.

The competition was so vehement and so successful, in other words, that each community managed to chase away the project from the other. If they had both exhibited a passive refusal to cooperate with one another it might have meant one community would have received the project anyway. In that case success would have spilled over into the neighbouring community and eventually they might have realized that they could work together and both could benefit. Indeed, if they had started off cooperating they might have landed that construction plant and perhaps other growth projects in the future, thereby solidifying long term economic success for them both. Instead, that active competition meant that both communities got to enjoy the sweet smell of failure, both their own and that of their neighbour. Their dedication to competing in such a fashion ensured the combined failure of the region, and thanks to the reputation they now have, it has ensured failure for many years to come.

I must clarify here that there is a distinction to be made between the competition I so openly embraced and discussed in Chapters 2 and 5 and the competition that I am rather critical of in the preceding paragraphs. In all cases the competition is vigorous, but in the earlier chapters the competition is for the betterment of the community as a whole, while the type of competition I have discussed in this chapter benefits no one, and invariably brings about failure. There are clearly times when competition is healthy and times when cooperation is the best method for success. Competition in individual sports such as boxing or golf is the only way those sports work, since a cooperative approach would drastically reduce ticket sales and viewership. Parents are successful when they cooperate in raising children, but it would not be successful if parenting were based on competition. Hockey players must do both, but they must do each at the appropriate times or they fail. As players and as a team they compete against other teams and if they play the best they can as players and play within a team cooperatively, they can win. If they compete against players on their own team, however, then they will fail collectively as a team and will fail in competition against other teams. Clearly there are times that competition is healthy and necessary and there are times when we must realize as a team that we must all work together cooperatively or we will all fail. As the saying goes, "we can either work together, or we can hang alone."

I have discussed how passively refusing to cooperate can assist in killing your community, and how actively competing against other groups or communities can complete the job to perfection. Passively refusing to cooperate means that others will simply carry on with their business as usual and should they have success it will likely spill over into your group or community whether you want it to or not. Actively engaging in competition can ensure that you and other communities and groups expend valuable resources in fighting each other, which can help ensure their reduced success or outright failure, which in turn can aid in your desire to fail. In that case, however, other communities or organizations may simply choose to avoid your community or organization altogether.

If passive and active non-cooperation are not effective enough for you, however, and you want to be *absolutely* assured of failure for yourself and others, there is still another technique you can harness in your campaign to kill your community. This is the "volunteer vampire." Initially I didn't believe the stories I had heard about this malignant force, even though the testimony was compelling, until I personally bore witness to it myself. Since then I have listened closely and sought out other stories. I have realized my initial impression that such a mythical beast couldn't exist was wrong, but wrong too was my understanding that such a creature must be the rarest of all life forms. I have heard testimony from community after community confirming that volunteer vampires exist, they exist in large numbers, they exist in every community, and they live right out in the open with the rest of us. They are the most devious and harmful troublemakers in our communities, yet they are often celebrated as saviours. If you really want to kill your community you can skip over the initiative to not cooperate, slide on past the desire to compete, and move right on to become a volunteer vampire.

To be a volunteer vampire you must seize any initiative that requires leadership and then, in that capacity, you have to suck the life out of every idea and action that is suggested that could get the project successfully completed. In many cases I have witnessed or heard of, a volunteer rises to the challenge and takes on a project that the community so desperately needs. They always place themselves as the ultimate champions of the drive or cause that needs to be realized. They rally the troops, they build a team, they are virtually inseparable from the project itself. They have a dedicated base of supporters who proclaim the greatness of the vampire and often assert that if the project can't be done by that particular person then it can't be done at all.

From that moment on, as community volunteers rally and begin work on the project, the vampire sucks the life out of each and every idea and drains the life out of every hopeful volunteer. For example, someone might suggest the idea of having a fundraising supper. The volunteer vampire, pointing out how many other events the supper would be competing against, convinces the others that the idea should not even be tried. Or an idea will be presented to apply for some government or community grants as a way of raising funds; the volunteer vampire will point out how long and complicated and time-consuming those forms are, how you will be competing with larger centres that pay professionals to fill out those forms and chase grants, so the energy expended on that would be fruitless. An idea will be presented to simply have a door-to-door fundraising drive; the volunteer vampire will point out that the volunteer base in the community is already exhausted with countless other projects, how people are tired of always giving to everything every evening on their doorstep, and how the downturn in the economy or the crisis in agriculture means everyone is broke and has no money to spare no matter how good the cause. In other words, the very idea is foolish and the effort would be a waste of time and energy. A closely related volunteer vampire technique is to ridicule or undermine the ideas and accomplishments of other volunteers, especially if those ideas and accomplishments threaten to outshine the vampire's own contributions.

And so every idea and every volunteer will be picked off one at a time as though in some low budget horror movie, except the deaths are slow and withering and devoid of the classical screams. The life, blood, and soul of the entire project and everyone involved are sucked out by the volunteer vampire. Eventually the project dies. However, since every argument was built on a grain of truth and every reason was very sound and logical, though negative, there is no sadness or sense of despair in the end. Rather, there is almost a sense of relief as though a diseased animal has been relieved of its earthly bonds rather than being allowed to suffer a slow and painful death. No deceased hope is mourned. Instead, the volunteer vampire is often celebrated as someone who tried against all odds to accomplish something that turned out to be impossible. In Omegatown, in a case that I witnessed myself, the volunteer vampire came very close to having a day named after her in the community until she was exposed in the light as having never actually accomplished a single project that she was involved in. She was one of the most skilled volunteer vampires I have ever witnessed.

Let's summarize. Killing your community is a very easy task to accomplish. The question of your success often depends only on the amount of energy and time you wish to expend in achieving that goal. Passively refusing to cooperate takes very little work over the short term, but does require continued focus to ensure that you maintain the same attitude time after time with group after group or community after community. Better still, try aggressively competing with other organizations or communities. This does take more time and attention over the long term, but if you can induce neighbouring communities to develop an unfriendly attitude that will sabotage any future opportunities that might come to your own community, the results will be well worth your effort. If you have time on your hands, though, and a focus for detail, and you wouldn't mind being celebrated for killing your community, becoming a volunteer vampire will allow you to suck the life out of each individual person, idea, and project that may arise. This requires both short term and long term commitment, but in the end, if killing your community is what you seek, then you have simply got to devote that extra time required to do the job right.

Chapter 8
Live in the Past

As I said at the beginning of this book, killing your community is all about attitude. Some people will suggest that if the hospital gets closed your community will die. Others suggest that if you lose a couple of grades at your school to the neighbouring town, that will do the job. Still others seem to suggest that the survival of your community is dependent on whether or not a road is built around your town, or whether you get a new soccer field or ball diamond. I agree that those infrastructure elements are important as a foundation to build upon, but none of them, not even closing your hospital, can make a life or death difference all by itself. I have witnessed hospitals open and close and have yet to see one kill a community – or ensure its success, for that matter. In fact, some of the fastest growing, most successful communities I have seen don't even have a hospital and never had one. No, those elements are *not* the beginning and end of a community. The beginning and end of every community is its people and the collective attitude they have about how they define success and whether or not they want to achieve it.

Attitude is what communities live and die by, and few of those attitudes are more successful at killing a community than the one that has you always living in the past. Almost everywhere I speak I have a conversation with someone who displays this attitude overtly, though they seldom seem to realize it. Often, after I present my speech, someone who displays this attitude will come up to talk to me. I always ask them if they were listening to the part of the speech when I talked about "living in the past" and they always say, "yes, that was excellent" and then carry on with comments and questions that are a perfect example of what I had just suggested they should avoid. It is a common human trait to hear information we consider valuable and then apply it to everyone else we deal with in our daily lives but fail to apply it to ourselves. Self-reflection for the purpose of improvement is a hard skill to learn and hard for the ego to accept.

People generally display this type of attitude in one of two ways. The first way is to hold on to the glory of the past. Generally those in this category see the past through a romantic, or at least nostalgic, lens that idealizes some very non-ideal elements of history. Many books and films have romanticized the Middle Ages, or the Victorian age, or the roaring 20s, or the cool 50s. They will capture the age by capitalizing on some aspects that are interesting or colourful, while ignoring those less appealing details in order to draw the reader or watcher – or themselves – into the fantasy. The Middle Ages can look romantic, even attractive, when portrayed without the infrequent opportunities for baths, rampant head lice, and rats that led to the black plague. The roaring 20s seem like an ideal and exciting time when you ignore the low wages and absence of safety measures and health-care. Any age can be very idealized by simply removing the bad stuff. The human mind is a power machine and, for the sake of self-preservation, has a discreet way of removing many elements of pain while saving to memory all those wonderful moments that make us smile.

As a result, our own past is often a powerful picture of happiness and success and contentment. It is a romanticized movie of our own lives, in which we idealize the clothes, the cars, the houses, the friends, and the good times that we had. Our memories are often much less complicated than our experience of the present and our instinct about the future, and so we tend to look back with fondness on the simpler days that are now behind us. Typically the older we get the less we look forward to the complexities of the future and the more we long for the simplicity of the past. I know one man who still says that he is not buying into these computers since they are just a gadget phase that complicates our lives and they will go away. We know they won't go away, and so does he, but many of us at one point or another have realized that technology has not made our lives simpler, and we sometimes question whether we use technology, or technology uses us. As such, there is often an unconscious desire to return to the good old days, the days when life was simpler, moral decisions were straightforward and obvious, we were all happier, and our communities were strong.

We all feel this way at one time or another; sometimes, if the feeling becomes overwhelming, it seems that the only way to correct the problems we see around us is to undo some or most of the modernization of the last few years. To make our communities strong and stable for the future we need to blow up some of those great roads we built that allowed everyone to leave town to go shopping elsewhere. To make our communities strong and stable for the future we need only bring back the ice cream parlours and get rid of the supermarkets that took people off our streets as families and put them into buildings as consumers. To make our communities strong and stable for the future we need only bring back door-to-door milk delivery, drive-in movies, and Buick Skylarks and all will be better. I personally believe that transforming our communities should begin with reintroducing the front porch, but that may be my own personal sentimentalism setting in. The fact is, we cannot simply return to the past, and even if we could, I doubt everything was as dreamy and wonderful as we remember it. The world is moving and changing. Spending countless hours discussing the glory of the past distracts us from the real and meaningful discussion about the future and how our community life fits in to it.

One of the challenges our communities face is that we have not candidly discussed what we want them to look like in the future. We have replaced front porches and ice cream parlours with large basement theatre rooms and secluded, fenced-in back yards, but we have done little to define the nature of these new communities and how they should be developed in this age of cocooning. So we lament our losses and indulge in nostalgia for the past, but we have not made the transition for the future. As a result, it is commonplace in a discussion about the re-invention of communities to discuss the glory of the way things used to be. In reality that only serves to help kill our communities, as lamenting the past accomplishes nothing and just interferes with making plans to meet the challenges of the future. Extended interludes of reflection can leave us all feeling defeated about the future, short on hope, and slightly lost.

People who live in the nostalgia or romance of the past are excellent at draining the energy of creative, forward thinkers. They are excellent at getting people with ideas to lose track and become defeatist in their thinking, thereby leading to failure before any project or idea gets off the ground. They convince others, sometimes unconsciously, that things will never be as good as they were and that there is no point in doing something new because everything only takes us farther off the track and further away from all that used to be right in our communities. Everything needs to be undone, they will claim. Such people are most adept at changing the conversation from the search for solutions for the future to a sterile fixation about the glory of yesterday, a glory that is often a romanticized distortion of what the past was actually like.

During one Omegatown visit I met a very wonderful and happy man who seemed to really like the "13 Ways to Kill Your Community" speech I had given. He expressed how proud he was to know that the future was in such good hands with young men like me. He spoke of how great his community *was*, how great it *was* to be able to spend his childhood in such a safe and happy town as his *was*, and how wonderful it *was* to have raised his children there. I assumed his age (he was 69) had led him to talk more in the past tense as he reflected on his life, and I reminded him that his town still was a safe place for kids and families to grow. He smiled and said, "No, it has all changed now that some of those big stores have come to town."

We talked at length about values and safety and happiness, and he insisted that the arrival of one store in that community had lead to a dozen more moving into town and setting up shop in the general vicinity, a scenario that is quite common these days. The man had a passion for his community and continued to volunteer in what seemed like half of the community's organizations. I felt bad for the fellow, whose entire town had changed and modernized on him in such short order and so recently – until I found out that the businesses that he was referring to, the ones that had changed everything so quickly from those glory days he remembered, had arrived eight years prior to that night I spoke.

I talked to numerous other people in the town that night who stayed around to chat, and many of them volunteered without prompting or leading questions from me that the elderly gentleman with whom I had talked was a beloved and kind man, but that he had opposed every change that ever took place in that community for over 40 years. Yes, you read that correctly. He was never vicious in his opposition, never started petitions, or spread lies, or gathered up hate. No, he was always kind, always smiling, and always talking about how the town was losing its sense of itself, how it was losing its glory, and how each new thing, from paving a street to tearing down an old building to putting up a new sign, was a change we would regret. He had great old stories about every ancient building, about every old tree, even about every old pothole – all the little features that made people feel at home in their community. His influence carried many along with him in opposition to every improvement, every modernization, every *whatever* that was being proposed. Eventually, however, a sense of ambivalence began to develop towards his unflagging opposition to every upgrade and innovation. His fellow townspeople all loved him, and they all hated him at the same time.

Not everyone holds onto the past with visions of glory and perfection, however. The majority of those who hold onto the past do so by identifying some historical wrong; they see every moment from that point forward as being a miscarriage of justice, and every moment into the future as a deliberately perpetrated mistake that will persist until the ancient wrong is fixed. While those who are merely nostalgic for the past are mistakenly taken as harmless romantics because of their personable and often friendly demeanour (which is deceiving – in actuality, such persons are not harmless at all), those who are looking for "justice" over a past wrong and stubbornly refuse to let it go are often overtly angry and hostile. They are the great grudge holders who feel someone or something wronged them, and everything in their life that has ever been bad or will go bad in the future can be tied to that one wrong. You may think I am exaggerating, but in the same visit to Omegatown I held a deep, extended conversation with someone of this nature that demonstrated to me the full validity of my claim. While the elderly gentleman I referred to above clung to the nostalgia of the community as it had been before that first large box business arrived and brought others with it, another person I met saw the presence of that store as a personal wrong that was done specifically to her.

This very angry lady suggested to me that the town council sold the land to the developer for a very low price and never gave any local business or entrepreneur an opportunity to purchase the land and then develop it. She was livid about that, and at first I believed she had every right to be. She also suggested that the store had stolen customers from all of the local businesses and that the business sector in town had all but shut down, meaning there were no local business owners left to employ people in town. She grew ever more livid as she spoke, and again, as with the older gentleman, I felt she was justified. I simply had to research what had transpired so I could talk about another way you could kill your community. Surely, I thought, this smiling gentleman and this entrepreneurial lady had cause to be concerned and upset.

I set to work on building a story around how the bringing in of this store had led to a weakening of the community, only to find out that both persons had told half truths and lies to me – and in all likelihood to themselves as well. The community had not had a glorious past before that one store showed up and brought others with it, as the smiling man had indicated. The town had lost two major industries and for almost 20 years teetered on the brink of collapse. Young people were fleeing because there was no work, the college had closed since all the young people had left, and businesses were shutting down. The land that was eventually purchased was advertised three times in three years, at a steal of a price, for locals to develop. No one ever made an offer. One local developer started a new value-added manufacturing industry that most people in town thought was a crazy idea, but it grew quickly and hired trained young people. That attracted a lot of young families back to the community within a couple of years.

As a result of the new economic activity, the box store that those two people detested purchased the piece of land for full market value, not the low price suggested by the angry lady. That in turn attracted more popular stores and businesses to the community. That in turn drew in shoppers from as far as an hour away, which I was told by many local business owners brought more money to town and revitalized the small business district, which lead to a new tax base that allowed lower property taxes, which encouraged many more people to choose the community to live in, which lead to many new housing starts. In other words, things started to improve with the new industry and that new box store. Not according to all, however, as one man felt a return to the past would be better, and another felt that some wrong was committed against her and it needed to be undone, and no good would every come until that perceived wrong was righted. That smiling face was compelling and hard to resist when I first heard the story. The outrage displayed by that lady was equally compelling and made me feel angry enough to get to the bottom of the scandal. I was momentarily ashamed when I realized the story was a sham.

Most often we see this behaviour and these attitudes manifest in comments that may seem minor. A committee is set up to work on some project and a comment is brought forward such as, "Oh that so-and-so's grandfather did something to my grandfather 42 years ago, so there's no way I can work with them ... ." There is always the very popular, "His father's uncle was a bit of a thief and a liar back in the 50s so if I were you I wouldn't get messed up in a project with him." Or, "Why would I help him now, when 30 years ago in high school he wouldn't help me with math, and he went out with the girl I liked ... what was her name again?" Or the most common, "Why should I help with that, what did you/ they/he/she/the community ever do for me?" That type of attitude is very prevalent in many communities. It is always centred on some long-held anger and a sense that life isn't fair and that you have been wronged in some way. If you are trying to build a strong community, that sort of attitude ensures that there is no sense of common ground on which to build. If you are trying to kill your community, however, that is exactly the sentiment you need to encourage.

Back in Omegatown many years ago, I was at a meeting to gather ideas about how to improve upon and build our communities for the rural development report I was writing. As usual I had invited a mixed group of about 20 people from all walks of life to ensure we had a free discussion on a multitude of topics. The report covered health, education, community infrastructure, economic development, youth, seniors, Aboriginals, tourism, arts and culture, water, infrastructure, transportation and trade, and the environment. We were working on ideas and trying to discuss ways that things could be improved when a man stood up and yelled at me, "Nothing will get better until natural gas prices are reduced." I suggested that was a legitimate issue but it should not stop us from talking about all the other issues that could and should be discussed now about the future of our communities as we looked at a solution to the high price of natural gas. He interrupted, "No, nothing you do will make one bit of difference until you fix that natural gas situation." Natural gas pricing had been de-regulated 20 years earlier and this seemed to be a thorn in his side as we tried to discuss other issues.

I finally had to ask him to leave, as his outbursts and anger were distracting from the purpose and focus of the meeting. He was doing an exceptionally good job of stopping us from talking about anything that dealt with the present or the future. He wanted to discuss the past and nothing else. He wanted to prevent everyone else in the room from thinking about the future, about future developments, about solutions and options, about what might come, and about how to transform our communities. All he wanted was to talk about what he felt was an injustice from the past – he was convinced that nothing good could ever happen until justice had been served. Given his anger and how long he had been holding onto it, it seemed obvious that his own life had been held ransom by the issue and that he would not know how to move on even if his issue were resolved.

I always try to be fair and honest when dealing with those who hold such grudges that infect their comments, their attitude, and their chance for success, but I have become more and more frank as the years wear on, with less and less patience for such negativity and the impediments to progress it throws up. Quite simply, I don't care to dwell on old, uncorrected wrongs. We are supposed to learn from the past, and I do, or at least I try to. I study the past and read history voraciously because it is imperative that we understand it so that we do not repeat its mistakes, but we are not supposed to live in the past. When the past becomes an impediment to our growth, our development and our future, then it has wedged its way too far into our lives and we have to move on, move over, or move beyond it.

Wrongs have always been committed, mistakes have always been made, and that will always be the case whenever people set out to accomplish something. My grandpa always used to say that the only time you don't make a mistake is when you do nothing. As much as we need to correct the wrongs, at some point we need to move on to discuss solutions, not talk incessantly about what wrong was committed. Mistakes happen, but solutions don't make themselves happen. You have to work on solutions for the future, and that only happens when you let go of mistakes, and the glory of the past. I don't want to be rude, but there isn't enough time to dance around with niceties. The future of our communities across North America is at stake, not its past. Those who wish to see our communities succeed for our children need to deal with persons who want to work for the future. If you spend your whole time looking backwards, you have no idea where you are going and you are sure to get there.

The attitude that causes someone to live in the past, whether it is holding on to the idea of some glorified Utopia, or holding on to some injustice that must be righted before anyone can move ahead, keeps everyone looking in the wrong direction. That type of thinking detracts from every project, initiative or investment that will help build your community's future. Albert Einstein said, "Learn from yesterday, live for today, hope for tomorrow." It is a valuable quote to hold on to. If you want to kill your community, live in the past. If you keep people thinking about the past, you can be sure they will forget about their future and the future of their community.

Chapter 9
Ignore Your Seniors

Seniors are an important element in any society and their importance grows, as do their numbers. In many cultures around the world seniors are revered for the wisdom and experience they hold. Most of us, however, tend to view our seniors as just easy-going and cordial folks. They are rarely viewed as a factor when it comes to the future. Don't be fooled. They are a dangerous group that under the right circumstances can cause a riot of success. Seniors across North America have two important assets, and have them in a greater abundance than the average citizen within the general population: time and money. These are key factors in building a successful community, so it is critical that you do everything in your power to relegate seniors to the sidelines if you wish to ensure the failure of your community.

Most communities have what I often refer to in my rural development work as the STPs, the Same Ten People. Often it's the same small group of people who sit on the town or county councils, run their business or work their job, coach a sports team, lead charitable organizations, volunteer at the school, mentor in scouts and put away the chairs at church. It was amazing, the number of times I would attend meetings with different groups over different issues, only to discover as the day and evening progressed that each time I left one meeting it was almost the same group of people that joined me at the next meeting over a different issue. I would speak with the school parent council, the town council, and the library board all over varying issues. Each time we would all leave the first meeting to move on to the next one twenty minutes or so later only to find most of the same faces re-assembled. The STPs are the people who help keep the community going because of all of the capacities in which they serve. Without those volunteers on so many different organizations, committees and groups it seems unlikely the community would last long at all. That is how important volunteers in a community are to its development and growth.

When seniors retire they suddenly find they have time on their hands. Most of the rest of us are still working one or two jobs, raising the kids, running them to all sorts of events, volunteering at organizations, and so on. Seniors have freed themselves from many of those bonds and are looking to enjoy life; after all, they helped to build the communities we live in and have earned a little time off. Just because they've retired from their careers, however, does not mean they are ready to stop volunteering forever. They want to keep building for their grandchildren and great grandchildren's benefits. Sure, seniors may take a break from many of those activities so they can travel a bit more and golf a bit more, or whatever else they were planning to do when they retired, but seldom do they go so far they can't find their way back. They want to continue to help and volunteer. They want to visit with their friends and spend time helping in the community. They want to be useful and they want to feel needed. We all do. And like everyone else, sometimes they feel relegated to the background, like they are not needed or wanted. If that happens, sometimes they feel it is hard to get back into the circle they once occupied, and so they watch from the outside in. Sometimes the seniors need to be asked seven times, like youth do, before the barrier breaks down and they feel like they are still welcome as active members of the community. More often, however, all it takes is a phone call asking them if they are willing to help, and then they will be back in droves, making their voices heard and making new and meaningful contributions.

Successful communities often capture that senior resource and have an excellent senior volunteer base for many functions and organizations. Some communities have gone as far as hiring a volunteer coordinator to identify and recruit volunteers and match them with the proper organization. The coordinator can help ensure that volunteers' time is properly managed, that the experience is enjoyable, that the greatest efficiency possible is achieved, and that volunteers are not burning out. That is particularly important to seniors who want to do something enjoyable, want opportunities to visit and meet new people, but don't want to be over-used and don't want to be turned off volunteering. Communities that successfully recruit volunteers also realize the advantages of building cross-generational relationships and benefit from the power those relationships have for the betterment of the community as a whole. They realize that mixing and blending youth, seniors, and those ages in between serves up an incredible depth of experience and transference of knowledge, energy and ideas. Those communities are successful. If you are looking to kill your community, make sure at all costs that you avoid senior recruitment in volunteer organizations.

The second element that seniors bring is money. I want you to understand right now that I am not suggesting that you get those seniors to invest in every hare-brained scheme that you come up with, and hound them to donate to every fundraising cause and event you can dream up. I have in mind something much different than that. If you read the news and listen to the media you may get the impression that all seniors are poor and destitute. That is simply not true. There is no doubt that some are poor, but there are a lot of seniors in our communities who are comfortably wealthy. If seniors didn't have money there wouldn't be cities like Phoenix, Arizona, the entire state of Florida, or communities like Camrose, Alberta that have grown and achieved success because seniors have chosen to live there for all or part of each year.

Those communities have something to offer, such as a lot of sun, but many have taken some of that natural capital and added many other elements that attract seniors. Often the warm weather is the initial attraction, but if that were the only draw then why would some places stand out over others that offer similar weather? The answer is that some communities enhance their attractiveness by adding other services and elements to maximize their draw. Some have made available more appropriate housing. Others offer features such as laundry service, or offer specific entertainment such as square dancing. In fact, one senior told me that he and his wife live half the year in a small community outside Apache Junction, Arizona and the other half in the community of Viking, Alberta. They chose Alberta and Arizona because those places have a high number of sun days and lots of heat, but at manageable levels at the times of year they are there. They chose those particular towns because they both offered square dancing. As regions, Alberta and Arizona rank as having the greatest number of sunny days on the continent, but as communities, Viking and Apache Junction had the services to draw that couple to them.

Some successful communities have realized the opportunities to capitalize on natural assets that attract seniors. This can involve developing services around laundry and transportation, entertainment such as camping, golfing and dancing, gambling and appropriate meals, or anything else that seniors demand. Whatever the attraction might be, those communities have realized that seniors are not what the typical stereotype imagines them to be. Too often we collectively imagine seniors simply as people who are waiting to die, but in reality seniors are people who are just about to start living life to the fullest. At the age of 65, most seniors who are fully retired have freed themselves from the obligations of daily life that so many of us are bound by with work and raising kids. They are going to do what they want to do, and since many of them have some funds saved, they are able and willing to pay for it.

Realizing that seniors are consumers who have some money and a desire to get the greatest enjoyment out of life can lead to an immense wealth of new ideas about what they are seeking and how to provide it. When new services and new entertainment are added to a community in order to give seniors a reason to stay, those communities often find that an interesting trend develops. Once seniors feel their needs are being met and they lose the desire to venture permanently to a different place, the word begins to spread and other seniors in different communities hear about the services and entertainment offered. Seniors will typically go wherever they need to get the services they desire, but usually, the less distance they have to travel the better. If they hear that a community not that far from theirs has great services of the type they are interested in, then they are more inclined to go there as a future place to live since it typically keeps them in relatively closer proximity to their grandchildren.

One of the biggest factors that so many communities, and business people, forget about when it comes to seniors as consumers is housing. Many seniors in our communities live in housing that is old and not modernized. Typically that is not an issue, except that most of those older designs have a lot of stairs and narrow doorways that are inappropriate for older people with bad knees or weaker legs, and completely inappropriate for anyone who requires a walker or wheelchair for mobility. As well, most of those seniors who raised families within those houses now find they have far too much space to heat and clean when there are only one or two people in the house. Potential reduced mobility issues are further amplified with large yards that require regular maintenance such as weeding and mowing. In short, many of our seniors find themselves in homes that have become inappropriate for a large variety of reasons, but typically they have owned the home for many years and have built up equity they are prepared to use.

In this context I recall a great discussion I had with a couple in their late 60s who lived in one of North America's largest and fastest-growing cities, Calgary. They had purchased their house 35 years earlier for less than one-tenth of what it was currently worth. Now their children had moved out and on, and lived in communities all across the continent. They lamented the fact that they used to know all their neighbours, they used to pay much less in property taxes, there used to be less crime in their neighbourhood, they used to be able to golf without an expensive membership at the golf club – in short, they had outgrown the size and style of their beloved home. I did not initiate the discussion, but since they had raised it I asked some simple questions through which I uncovered their key interests and established their reduced ties and loyalty to the neighbourhood and the city that had outgrown them.

It was like a revelation to them when I spoke of the dozens and dozens of communities not far from their current location that had condo-style living that was ideal for seniors, where they wouldn't have to mow the lawn or shovel snow, but they could still grow their garden, as they had for decades. They knew that senior-appropriate condos were available in some places, but they were not aware that many of the communities had beautiful places available for a fraction of the price they would pay in their current vicinity. Add to that the much lower property taxes and the strategic location near beautiful under-utilized golf courses that have very reasonable membership costs where you can usually just walk on instead of booking a time, and they were very intrigued. The clincher in the discussion occurred when I discussed the friendly nature of these communities, where they would get to know their neighbours, where they could feel safe and secure, and where they would be welcomed.

I got a call from them a few months later to inform me they had actually moved to a location they were thrilled with. I was delighted by their news, but I was not surprised by the community they chose, even though it was much farther away than I had imagined they would be willing to move. This community was, at one point not too many years ago, literally in the throes of death. The population was in rapid decline, the attitude of the remaining population was caustic, and businesses were closing up shop each month. The community could have been put on support systems to transition it through its remaining years and into a peaceful death. But then everything changed. A local entrepreneur transformed the entire face of that community with one action. The entrepreneur had observed that too many of her aunts and uncles and family friends were struggling with inappropriate housing as they aged. She spoke to everyone who was interested and compiled a list of persons ready to make a commitment, and then proceeded to build a condominium complex for those people, including herself, who wanted to sell their home and move into more appropriate housing. These people were not old and infirm. They simply wanted a place that was easier to clean, easier to get around in, and required less regular work and maintenance inside and out.

However, problems appeared. Despite the initial verbal commitment to the project, a few people were forced to back out or simply got cold feet so there were still some vacancies when the building was completed. The project was on the brink of unprofitability.

What happened next is an excellent example of the valuable economic stimulus that seniors from other communities can provide. Within a couple of months of the project's completion, two of the available remaining units were sold to people from out of town because nothing of the sort was available in their own communities for mature and senior people like themselves. When they saw that these units were still available at such a great price and right next to the golf course, they decided to move and take advantage of benefits that some persons in the community had failed to notice. Eventually word spread about the price of the units, their amazing layout, their proximity to the golf course and all the other services that the seniors wanted. Now, local residents as well as people from other communities began enquiring about future developments. The last I heard the developer was proposing another set of condominium units next door to meet the new demand from within and around the community.

The community at large had initially been indifferent to the project, and a few others were completely opposed when it was first suggested, mostly for reasons (discussed in other chapters) like jealousy, or small thinking, or opposition to business in general. Attitudes began changing when it became apparent that the new complex provided new business, investment and employment opportunities for the locals. A new clubhouse was built on the golf course, a new restaurant opened in town, a dry cleaning and laundry service opened, and then other businesses as more seniors moved in. A sense of excitement began to grow as more and more people recognized that the project – the largest in the community's history – had the potential to be followed by others. The next step in the community's re-growth, which was something that no one foresaw, was the influx of young families that began moving to the community. Some moved there to be closer to parents and grandparents or had heard about the job and business opportunities that were sprouting up. The town grew and developed into a place of opportunity for every generation and developed a culture and attitude of success. The caustic attitude was gone and people were moving back. I wasn't the least bit surprised that the senior couple I had spoken to had chosen this renewed old community.

Of course if your goal is to kill your community, then this sort of strategy is a drastic mistake. It is important to ensure that you don't offer the services and entertainment that seniors want as they move into the fun stage of their lives. In fact, don't even spend time figuring out what seniors are looking for or what they need – that way you can be sure that you will never provide those wants and needs and they will go somewhere else to get them. Be sure that you don't encourage housing, whether it is senior-appropriate condos, daily living assistance residences, or health-related housing projects. It is critical that you don't encourage the seniors to get engaged and active in the community organizations either, because regardless of whether they spend money in your community or not, they will still cause it to grow.

Even if you do build some housing that is adequate for seniors so they can stay in the community, it is important that you adopt the attitude that your seniors enter those places and never come out. Their goal at the age of retirement is to enter the appropriate facility to play shuffleboard and crib until they die. It will take diligence and dedication to keep them locked in. If you don't work hard at it they will sneak out and volunteer for something and become active because they helped build our communities and, frankly, still want to. However, to make really sure that you are getting rid of the influence any of your seniors may have, you must ensure that they don't have proper housing. If you are successful at this they will move elsewhere so your community can quietly die a slow death, while others grow because your seniors took their time and money with them when they left.

Chapter 10
Reject Everything New

The implicit nature in a human is to strive and work to achieve consistency because in consistency there is security. As we age this tendency increases and we become more willing to trade risk and adventure for security and consistency. On occasion the need for security and consistency becomes so strong that we willingly endure a harsh and bitter reality rather than take a risk to improve our fortunes. We tend to prefer the devil we know over the one we don't. This means that we often choose not to try new food, or new drinks, or new friends, or new places, or new ideas. We become entrenched in the status quo and what we know. As communities we often choose not to accept new people, or new ideas, or new ways of thinking, or new attitudes. We reject everything that is new and opt to keep the devil we know, the slow deterioration of our community, rather than the one we don't, even if the one we don't know holds potential for success, because we are afraid of change, even if the change may be success.

This truth initially became clear to me when I was first elected in April of 2002, as a bouncing new politician who was open to ideas and adventure and experience and learning. I was working very hard, crazy hours, always on the road, always at constituency events and almost living in my car in between. My parents got a bit concerned about me around October when I began to look a little run down even though I was revving and pulsing with excitement and energy and ready to take on the world. They insisted that I take a break, and so early in the new year I found myself on my way to a vacation in Mexico with my parents.

My parents are fantastic people who are still really quite young, we get along very well and I know and like all their friends. I greatly enjoyed the trip. We did a lot of touring of the countryside and the communities, sampled the culture and the food at local festivals, lounged in the sun on the beach or by the pool and generally had a lot of fun. Well, we all had fun except one gentleman. He wasn't really interested in the Mexican beach or the Mexican sun, the Mexican food, the Mexican culture, not even the Mexican beer, and honestly, he was pretty down on everything that we experienced. None of us let that bother us, but I wondered why he was there. I asked my dad one evening why a guy who seemed to dislike everything about Mexico bothered to come there in the first place.

My dad explained that the gentleman actually wanted to try to do something different, but because he'd never ventured beyond the sight of the water tower back home he had no idea what he was in store for. I suddenly had a very clear picture of a man who had literally never lost sight of the water tower. Obviously, it didn't work out for him. He was unable to forget what he was used to, couldn't open up his mind to the new situation and the new environment, and so he couldn't enjoy the experience. Instead, he just grumbled about how he didn't like "it" and "it" was everything. Now, it wasn't really his fault because after almost 70 years of the same old same old, with very little experience at sampling new things, it really was bound to be incredibly difficult to enjoy trying something new.

I was reminded of this story some years later as I was giving a speech that included some very off-the-wall ideas for igniting a fire (figuratively speaking) in rural communities. I had finished the speech and was taking questions from the floor when one man raised his hand and said, "You can't really expect us to try one of those ideas you mentioned?" I shrugged and told him he could try something else if he wanted to and then asked him why he didn't think the community could try one of those ideas. He said, "Well, we have never tried them before." Yes, he said those exact words. My mind instantly flashed to the elderly man in Mexico who had never tried anything new and wasn't about to start now. I tried to hide the insidious smirk on my face as I reminded him of a quote from Alberta Einstein, "The definition of insanity is doing the same thing over and over again and expecting different results each time." Why not give something new a shot, especially since the tried and true ideas haven't succeeded yet?

I felt bad for that gentleman in Mexico because he hadn't experienced other cultures when he was younger and had very rarely tried anything completely new, if ever. I found myself thinking about the difference between people who never had the chance to experience other cultures and people who never took that chance when the opportunity was presented to them. Both live in very small worlds with little variation in their experiences, which means they are both ignorant of the diversity of life and lifestyles around the globe. One, however, is a victim of circumstance because the choice is not theirs, while the other is the engineer of their own ignorance and must accept full responsibility because they choose not to experience new things. Historically it is conceivable that many of our small communities were victims of circumstance, but now, in this modern day and age, many are passive engineers of their own limitations.

In terms of rural development and community growth, many years ago there was very little information available to assist communities looking for ideas. Many communities even refused to share information and stories with one another about their successes and failures. The larger challenge, however, lay in where to find the information that was shared. Communication was very poor compared to what it is now. Younger readers will probably not recall that only two generations ago many farmers and rural residents did not have phones for the first thirty years of their lives. Now, as every young person knows, we have instant video communication to and from the rest of the world. I can video conference with friends in Korea for free, I can view towns' websites from around the world and I can peruse research from thousands of universities on any continent on the globe.

There are rural development institutes that perform research on the viability of rural and small communities in most countries of the world. Free university research is readily available about sustaining small communities and the importance of, and ways to maintain, rural economic regions. Communities are setting up websites to post their own success stories and models for long term prosperity, and to advertise their own success. These examples are readily available, are free for the taking, and are simply waiting for you to come along and apply them to your situation. I emphasize this because trying to come up with ideas to ensure the viability of your community does not mean that you and you alone must devise some brilliant, amazing, creative, revolutionary, "never-even-been-conceived-of-before" idea that you can apply to your community in order to ensure success. Sure it would be wonderful if you did, but you really don't have to reinvent models for success when there are so many that can be borrowed.

I'm reminded of a friend from my first year of university (we became even better friends when we both failed out of that first

year and the next year found ourselves at the same college working on redemption). We did a lot together that second year and
spent a lot of time hanging out, except for the spring break week.
He went off to some spring break town to have a good time and
I went home to work on the farm. When he got back he was
very worked up and quickly told me how he was going to quit
school and start his own business and make a lot of money, and
that I should get into the business too, and we had to start right
away and the opportunities were endless. He was very excited.
He explained that he had found the perfect business idea when
he was on vacation.

The spring break period at our college didn't quite coincide with
the spring break from other institutions so my friend had a few
quiet days in that community after the parties were all over. He
explained how he was sitting on a patio one afternoon and noticed
that the business across the street was as busy after the students
had left as when they were there. In his words, "people were going
in there steady to drop money and it didn't seem to matter what
was going on or what time of day it was." He realized that the
community he was visiting for spring break was quite similar to
the one he planned on living in back home. They were of similar
size and population distribution, and had a similar economic
base, yet, he explained, the community back home did not have
a business at all like the one he was watching. His notion was to
set up the same business at home. If it works here, he reasoned,
it had to work there.

He took that idea and headed home to begin his new enterprise,
which has been a huge success for him and for the community he
built it in. Now he has three of those identical businesses. He spends
a lot of time touring throughout the U.S. and Canada identifying
businesses that are stellar successes, seeking out communities that
lack that proven successful business, and then replicating them

in those communities. He always does his homework correctly and completely and has a perfect record of success. On occasion it did bring a sigh to my lips when I climbed back into my five-year-old Chevrolet Impala after a cup of coffee with him and watched him drive off in his very nice, very new Jaguar. I used to lament that moment I turned down the opportunity to join him in his business venture, but I have since learned that we all have roles to play and that mine is to help small communities find success because that is where my passion leads me.

Every time we have coffee he reminds me that his realization that day on the patio was not about the successfulness of that particular business, but about how successes were all around him, staring him in the face. His insight was that many wonderfully creative people had taken risks to try out something new and all he had to do was learn from their success and mimic it elsewhere. Sure, you can criticize him for not being original, but ideas are borrowed all the time. The first people with ideas for a grocery store, a hardware store, a pharmacy and so on, had their ideas copied and improved upon. It is common in business. The only real difference in this case is that the models were borrowed, slightly improved upon, and then set up in a location where there was no competition and in a place where it was quite clear that the business would be a success because it had already been a success in a near-identical place. One of my favourite quotes comes from him: "People always talk about learning from other people's mistakes and failures. I find it much more prudent and profitable to learn from other people's successes."

There are stories of success from communities all over the world eager to share their experiences. It's there for you to see, all you have to do is try something new. It may not be something that has never been tried before, but honestly, why take the risk if there are so many different examples of ideas that have already been proven successful and simply need to be slightly modified and adapted to your particular community? If you're a medium sized community that sits at the edge of a mountain range, for instance, and you are wondering about ways to improve your community, there are bound to be thousands of communities similar to yours that have tried and succeeded with ideas that you would never have dreamed of yourself, but which would fit very successfully into your community. It doesn't matter if you are large or small, near a lake, on the prairie, surrounded by forest, or situated on a river. Some community that may be thousands of miles away is in a similar situation and has tried and succeeded with ideas that will work for you and your community. All you need is a computer, some patience and a willingness to try something new.

This does not mean that you should completely give up on looking for truly new ideas that are unique to your community. Of course, you may discover something that absolutely no community on Earth (at least that you know of) has ever tried before. It is always worth a shot to try something new when you have confirmed that everything you have tried before has not worked. Presenting new ideas for consideration may possibly make you a target of ridicule and criticism, but you have got to be willing to take the risk. Every great and wonderful invention, every discovery, every idea or change in the course of human history whether it was global or local, originated with someone who was ready to take a risk. If no one took a risk or took a chance just because they could fail or be ridiculed, then nothing would ever change. It would be status quo until the end of time.

When I was a high school student I was invited to participate in a series of three discussions about the future of the community. Throughout the second meeting we were discussing ideas for attracting people and their money. It was nearing the end of the meeting before I finally built up my courage to offer what I believed to be a meritorious idea. The town I grew up in is a very lovely little community that sites bravely in the middle of an extensive expanse of table-top prairie. I cautiously raised my hand and offered up tourism as an idea to attract people and money to the community. A much more experienced gentleman snickered and bleated, "What are they going to come and do? Watch the dog run away for three days?" His put-down wasn't meant to insult me but rather the supposedly unalluring environment in which our community was located. Regardless, it bit me hard and I sat meekly and made no comment the rest of the meetings.

I had the notion that someone, somewhere in such a large world would want to see something that we had to offer. I was also convinced that if just the odd busload of people showed up and walked around snapping a few pictures, then others in the town would start to wonder what they found so interesting. I thought perhaps if a few tourists took an interest and an appreciation in the community and its surroundings, some of the people in town might do the same. Rarely do we appreciate what we have until someone else appreciates it. There would be nothing like a few tourists stopping in every week, taking pictures and talking and pointing, to remind everyone in town that what they have is of interest and should not be taken for granted.

I did not know exactly how or why tourists would come to the community, but I thought it was a worthy idea to raise at a meeting designed to dream up ideas for the community's future. I thought it was an idea that could and should be explored and if it had no merit then so be it, but it had never been thought of before so it was worth a shot. I discovered much later on, after a tour through Germany, that Germans are fascinated with Western culture. German authors wrote many "Old West" books in the German language and German artists travelled the West in the 1800s, painting Native American life, and out of those pursuits grew a fascination with the "Wild West" mystique. Clubs have been formed that have Western-themed parties where people dress up as cowboys and Native Americans – but finding authentic clothes for such an occasion was almost impossible. What a business opportunity! Regular blue jeans stitched with Native American designs and tapestry would fetch a ten-fold increase over the price of the jeans alone. Sadly, nobody took advantage of the idea.

Years after that elder gentleman had discounted my tourism suggestion and I learned of German interest in Western culture, I looked around and saw a frontier prairie outpost surrounded by old-fashion cowboys who ran cattle and buffalo. I saw a town with an authentic steam train that still ran for local tourists, a river close by that offered canoeing and hiking, and picturesque views of expansive wind-swept native prairie. There is no doubt that not every German has that fascination with western culture, but there are eighty-seven million of them. It would only take a few to turn that small prairie town on its ear and cause the locals to wonder what the tourists saw and to appreciate what the tourists came to appreciate.

I now find it humorous when an idea I present is ridiculed before it is ever explored because I immediately imagine someone sitting on a beach complaining that they don't like being made to enjoy the warm sun, the soft breeze, and the cool beer because they have never tried it before. People who suggest trying something new are often ridiculed or resented because everyone hates change when it is first presented. Often times, after the change has occurred and everyone gets used to it, however, they act as though it has always been that way and defend against any new change, good or bad, for the sake of securing the new status quo. I have seen a lot of successful communities that have built themselves up with creative, unique ideas, but I have also seen a lot of communities that have "borrowed" others' successful strategies. Communities that seek out ideas, that explore options, and find partners that extend beyond the sight of the water tower often find an entire new world of opportunities on which they can capitalize. They find the future.

Communities that run from new ideas out of fear, that shun opportunities that stare them right in the face from across the street, that embrace everything that's old, that's tired, that's worn out, all with their proven recipes for disaster – these are the ones that are truly committed to achieving failure. If failure of your community is what you are after, don't consider any new ideas. Abandon the notion of taking a risk with something unproven because the chance that something might happen to change the course of your town's future to the good is too great. If failure of your community is what you seek you should especially turn away from any ideas that have already proven to be a success in other places. Those types of ideas come with little risk and high reward and could easily transform your community. It is of critical importance in achieving a desirable level of failure that you never let your minds wander beyond the sight of the water tower, never let ideas come from a vantage point further away than where they came from in the past, and simply continue to do the same things you have always done over and over and over. With proper focus and dedication your community can slowly go insane and die doing exactly what it has always done time and time again.

Chapter 11
Ignore Outsiders

In previous chapters we have discussed the qualities and values that specific groups bring to your community. Youth bring energy and ideas, seniors often bring time and money, but frequently both groups are ignored or under-utilized, which is truly an exceptionally effective way to kill your community. Those are not the only two groups that are important to ignore if you are looking to bring about failure, however. If you wish to kill your community it is important to identify all persons who could be classed as outsiders and keep them on the periphery of your organizations, clubs, and plans for the future.

Outsiders have many common traits, but they are not one distinct group. Outsiders are those who do not typically identify with your community's shared general sense of who it is. Outsiders can be from a different, distinct cultural group, or speak a different language, have a different history, live a different lifestyle and eat different food, or anything else that makes them different from the average member of your community. For the sake of clarification but also for brevity I will be discussing two different types of outsiders in this chapter: those from another community within

North America, and those who came to North America from a very different type of cultural base. Both groups present unique assets that can cause success – they must therefore be carefully kept from playing any important role in your community. In your campaign to prevent outsiders from making positive contributions, it is helpful to understand the role each group can play.

The first group that we will discuss are fellow countrymen and women who were not born in your community. They may come from 30 miles down the road, or they may in fact come from 3,000 miles across the country, but they are outsiders to your community nonetheless. They are outsiders because often very little is known about them by you or your community. They may stand out or they may blend in so well that at first blush you don't even recognize them as outsiders. Often the blending in is only on one side of the coin, however, and once you see the other side you will quickly recognize them as being outsiders who have moved into your community.

The reason that these outsiders are dangerous and can cause your community to experience success all comes down to the simple fact that they chose your community to live in. That's it, that's all. They chose your community for some reason, but the reason why they chose it is much less significant than the fact that they made the choice the way they did. They saw some strength that made them want to live there. Perhaps it was the job they wanted to take, perhaps it was the prime location for that business they wanted to start, or perhaps it is some quality of life factor that caused them to choose your community. The point is that they chose you. They chose your community as the place they will live, work, raise their family, spend their money, volunteer, and so on. In doing so, they will probably want to build your community up so they can improve the quality of life even further for themselves and their children. They could have gone anywhere, but they chose your community.

Those types of outsiders come to town without knowing who did what wrong to whose grandpa fifty years ago, or what family rivalries exist within the community, and they don't care. They are probably more interested in helping fix the sports facilities, volunteering at the school, painting old buildings, investing in a community park or playground, serving on town council and working or volunteering with the Chamber of Commerce or a similar organization. Interestingly, in many of the communities I have been to that have an economic or community development organization, it is primarily outsiders who are the members. The point is they are willing to help build your community because that is why they moved there, and they are completely unaware of your intent to destroy the very community they moved to.

In Omegatown I met a family who had lived in the community for 17 years. They moved from another community only two hours to the south of their present location. The country was the same, the language hadn't changed, and the street signs were identical. The family drove the same makes of cars as the locals, spoke using the same slang expressions as the locals, and worked at the same types of jobs as the locals. The family had moved to the new community for the better schools, the better sports programs, and the higher quality land that was available for lower prices than where they had moved from. That was all of their motivation. Apparently the purchase of the land upset a few locals who were eyeing the property but would not commit to the price being asked, and apparently a few more locals were upset by the fact that the newcomers' three boys were all exceptional athletes and stood out in community sports activities. That was all it took. They were outsiders from the start and were still outsiders after 17 years. They never got invited to join clubs, never got asked to help volunteer, or fundraise, or donate, and were never really made to feel welcome, except by a very small group of fellow outsiders.

It seemed like a very sad story, but surely this must have been a rare exception?

Not so. Travelling around I discovered that every Omegatown is full of outsiders who are not new to the community but have lived there for significant periods of time, sometimes decades. They are shunned because they don't know the history of the community, or because they don't pay homage to the town's powerful families, or because they dare to challenge the status quo, but usually they are shunned because they took advantage of something the community offered that everyone else just took for granted. The land they bought – it was assumed – would eventually go down in price and someone local would buy it, or the locals' kids would always be the best athletes in their great sports programs, or no one would ever open up "that" business that turned out to be successful. The outsiders are usually entrepreneurial individuals who see an advantage of being a member of a community, capitalize on it, and then are shunned by the community that felt like the opportunity, the one they never took advantage of, rightly and justly belonged to them as the original town inhabitants.

If you want to kill your community you have to stave off the energy and ideas the newcomers bring, their commitment to building on your community's strengths and resolving its weaknesses. You need to keep them from serving on councils, committees, boards, or organizations that have an impact on your community's future. You need to ensure they don't feel welcome or included and don't blend into any social group. If you are lucky, their spirit will weaken and they will give up trying to help your community grow and improve. If you are really lucky and work hard they may grow so frustrated with the realization that your community is not what they thought it was that they move away, taking the remaining hope for success for your community with them.

This brings us to the second category of outsiders: the immigrant from another country. A book that has influenced my own thinking on this subject is *The Millionaire Mind* by Thomas J. Stanley. The book provides fascinating information and statistics that show the thinking and values of millionaires in North America, and explains what makes them become millionaires while the rest of us do not. I found it particularly interesting to discover that about half of all new millionaires in North America every year are first-generation immigrants who came here with virtually nothing. It is truly remarkable to realize that in one generation they've been so financially successful. Often, in the countries they've emigrated from, opportunities do not exist like those found here in North America. Often they have come without the education, without the work experience, without the language skills, all of which would be expected to put them instantly at a disadvantage over those born here in the land of plentiful opportunity.

Many of the immigrants who arrive on this continent have come from places where water, food and jobs are much more precious commodities than they are here. Often the type of school they go to is not an option because there is only one school – or no school at all. Often they come from places where there is no university or where they are excluded because of their class or status. They come from places where there is no universal health care, no vaccines and no such thing as a dentist. They come from places where there are no government grants or programs for education or for building sports facilities or policing. They come from places where they don't even have the right to vote, or if they do, they don't know if they are going to get shot or blown up if they try – but try and vote they do.

According to the "100 People on Earth" project, almost half the world's population lives without proper sanitation, one-third don't have a safe water supply, and thirteen percent are malnourished.

Although these facts are difficult to verify, the authors of the project also claim that one in five people in the world can't read or write, only two-thirds have a basic education, and ninety-seven per cent do not have a post-secondary education. Fully three-quarters of the people on earth have electricity, but for two-thirds of those people, having electricity means a lone light bulb hanging from the ceiling for evening light. Seventy percent of the world's population does not have a bank account. In fact, if you have a refrigerator with any food in it, a closet with some clothes in it, a bed to sleep in, and any kind of roof over your head, then you are richer than seventy-five per cent of the people of the world. If you add to that a sizable bank account and a thick wallet, you are now among the top eight per cent of the richest people on Earth. Fewer than one in ten people have anything approaching the rights and freedoms and opportunities that we often take for granted every single day.

This stands in startling contrast to the attitude of many persons born on this continent. We complain about how the government isn't doing enough, or providing enough, as we sit on our laurels and wait for somebody to do something for us. We have lost that entrepreneurial, adventurous spirit that our forefathers who came from other countries had, that spirit that built our communities without government grants and programs or consultants or feasibility studies and the like. We don't appreciate what it took to get here or what we have as much as we used to.

Immigrants come from places where self-reliance isn't just talked about in political circles and bragged about in coffee shops – it is the only option open to them, because there are no government grants for luxuries like sports facilities and community halls. They don't wait for someone else to do whatever needs doing, and don't spend a lot of time talking about what can't be done or how it is someone else's responsibility – they just get it done for themselves, their children and the future of their community.

They are willing to take what little they have, and risk it, and work incredibly hard for more because this is the only place they have ever known where that is actually possible and allowed. They wonder why we complain about good-paying jobs when they come from places with only menial jobs or no jobs at all. They wonder why we only get fifty per cent voter turnout at elections in a place that should celebrate freedoms the likes of which most of the world will never know.

I realized just how sad this mindset is when I discovered an example in Omegatown. Two grocery stores there had been successfully competing for years, a situation that benefited the entire community and the owners themselves. Then the owner of one of the grocery stores decided to sell his store and retire. He put the store up for sale and waited six months. Many locals expressed interest but no one would commit to purchasing it. Finally the store was bought by a family from another nation who moved to town to take advantage of a business opportunity they figured would be successful. I was shocked to hear the number of people who wasted hours of their lives complaining that the store had not been sold to a local buyer. The complaints had nothing to do with racism. There was no racism in that community or directed towards that family of new owners. The complaints were over the fact that an outsider bought the store. They all expressed appreciation that the store would have long hours and great service and bring in some new and interesting goods and foods, but they didn't like that the store was sold to outsiders. Even though the store sat there for six months for sale and no one moved to purchase it, they were upset that it wasn't sold locally. OK, maybe there was a touch of racism, but more likely it was ignorance and jealousy and stupidity all rolled into one.

Our communities were built by entrepreneurial families who travelled great distances in harsh circumstances to build lives, opportunities, and communities for their children and their grandchildren. Their spirit was a powerful force that transformed their insecure and dangerous way of life into the comfortable, stable, secure one we enjoy today. Their spirit is dead in us. We have grown fat and lazy and complacent and sit on the precipice of losing all that they struggled for and all we can do is sit in the coffee shop and complain that somebody else isn't fixing our little problems. We complain that there isn't a government grant to paint the slide when the community that surrounds that slide was created with sweat, faith, and the spirit of building a community that was born from our forebears. The only place that that spirit lives on is in the new immigrants that, true to the form of our founders, travelled great distances in harsh circumstances to build lives, opportunities, and communities for their children and their grandchildren. That entrepreneurial spirit, the desire to build more for the future, is what will carry us through and keep the engines of community-building fuelled.

If you want to kill your community, however, it is critical that you emulate a type of behaviour that doesn't welcome, engage, or support outsiders of any stripe, whether they are from out of town, out of the country, or just outside your generally travelled circles. Those outsiders bring fresh ideas, an entrepreneurial spirit and appreciation for your community and a desire to help build it for the future. Outsiders are a dangerous lot that are sure to cause success. The best way to deal with those people is to shut them out of all community organizations, shut them out of town and county councils, shut them out of successful business ventures and shut them out of economic and community development organizations. You may even want to consider spending time around town and in the local coffee shop talking about them and their "strange" outsider ways. Make them feel excluded and different, make people stare at them, and if you are lucky they will not only feel excluded but may in fact change their mind about your community and leave, thereby ensuring that the community continues to shrink in size in a closed-minded, closed-world way that will truly ensure your long term failure.

Chapter 12
Become Complacent

Regardless of how vigilantly we try to stay focused on our goals we can all lose sight of them momentarily and make mistakes that detract from what we want to achieve. Losing focus for a longer period of time can be dangerous to our long term success. We can't always be vigilant, but when we relax for too long we can lose focus enough that we forget how to regain it. That is when we become complacent, something that happens much more frequently that you would think. Many people who become complacent still talk a tough game and still give the impression that they are fully determined to attain their goal. Inside, however, they are often suffering from laziness, burnout, or overconfidence, but don't realize how their performance has been affected. Complacency is not as easy to recognize as you might expect, but is much more common than many people are aware. It is important, if you are going to ensure the death of your community, that you lose focus on your goals and become complacent, or support those who are complacent in their decisions and leadership roles within your community.

As I grew up, the greatest hockey team of the day, the decade and perhaps of all time was the Edmonton Oilers. Throughout the mid- to-late-1980s the Oilers had assembled one of the greatest rosters of hockey skill ever seen. Lead by the likes of Wayne Gretzky and Mark Messier, one of the greatest hockey talents partnered with one of the greatest sports leaders, the Oilers were in a league all their own. In the 1983-84 season they won their first Stanley Cup Championship handily. After two months into the 1984-85 season they had only lost three games and had won most of their games by huge multi-goal margins. They seemed to be a virtually unstoppable force of incredible skill. I remember watching Wayne Gretzky as he was interviewed after a game they had won 7 to 0. The interviewer summed up the situation well when he pointed out that the team was steamrolling the rest of the league, scoring record numbers of goals and heading for an almost unbeaten season. He suggested that the entire team must be pretty confident they were going to walk away with the Stanley Cup for the second year in a row. I will never forget the words that Wayne Gretzky told the interviewer.

"It is a lot of hard work to get to the top. It is even more and harder work to stay on top." As I was only 12 years old I didn't fully understand exactly what that meant, but the words burned into my mind. I knew that he meant it took hard work and focus to win enough games at the right time to ensure that they won the first Stanley Cup. I assumed the second part meant that everyone else in the league was gunning for you as last year's champions so you had to get better all the time, which was also true. It was a couple of years later before I understood the full implications of the second half of that quote. With such strength, with such skill, with such power, and with such a lead, it would be easy for the players to have assumed, just as the announcer had assumed, that they would automatically win the next Stanley Cup as well. It would have been easy for them to assume that they were miles ahead of the competition. The result would probably have been less effort in practice, less time spent focusing on the next game, fewer team-building exercises. The assumption that they would win again would have made them overconfident in their minds, which would have made them complacent in their actions. Eventually it would have caught up with them and they would have started to fall behind, started to lose games, and eventually would have been passed. It was hard work to become the Stanley Cup champions. Maintaining that lead the next year required even more work to avoid becoming complacent.

Communities too can experience problems that come from a similar sense of overconfidence. There are countless communities that have worked very hard for many years to make themselves beautiful, attract businesses, lure in young families, expand their recreational opportunities and build up a reputation for welcoming strangers. The community grows and builds and people begin to feel confident and secure. Eventually, and almost universally, that security and confidence becomes the dominant sentiment, overshadowing the desire to build and grow, and the town begins to retreat. It loses its focus on attracting young families, it stops succession planning for the future, it gets distracted from keeping itself attractive, it becomes selective about welcoming strangers, and it loses sight of the importance of attracting businesses. It becomes too wrapped up in its own sense of self worth and success, and communities that are still working very hard and are dedicated to being successful fly right on past. All that's left at that point is for the community to start to rebuild itself from the very beginning again, a prospect that is as long and hard to do as rebuilding a sports franchise.

Many communities say they are working to become sustainable. They do sustainability studies and undertake sustainability initiatives that are all part of some great sustainability plan. We use the word "sustainable" so much in community development

13 Ways to Kill Your Community

these days that I am not even sure what it means anymore. A dictionary definition might be "something that endures and maintains into the future." I believe that we have dropped emphasis on the "endures" part and put heavy emphasis on the "maintain." We have traded the concept that we have to put a lot of work and effort into building something that endures for the notion that we simply want to maintain unchanged what we have. That means that sustainable has become synonymous in many communities' minds with the words "status quo," which simply means keeping things as they currently are. Unfortunately there is no such thing as status quo when it comes to communities. The world and our communities are constantly changing and if we try to keep them just as they are we lose ground every day. We must constantly work hard at adapting to change just to keep our communities sustainably enduring. Instead, however, we often fight the forces of change, and work just to maintain and sustain what we have in more or less the form we have it. We try to keep the status quo.

As such, I would love to ban the word "sustainability" from the English language, or at least from use in the context of discussing community development. It has become a word like "nice" that seems to say something, but really says absolutely nothing about anything, or when on occasion it does mean something, it is usually warm oatmeal at best. I have told many communities that they should think of themselves as "dynamic," "vibrant," "adaptive," "responsive," "vigorous," "spirited," "virile," "resonant," "charismatic," "progressive," "vivacious," or any number of other near-synonyms that are a truer reflection of what they want their community to be – indeed, almost any adjective except "sustainable." Honestly, if a community is going to be sustainable, truly enduring into the future, it will need to be dynamic and vibrant and adaptive and responsive and vigorous and charismatic and so on and so on. That is what it means to be enduring. When communities only use the word "sustainable" these days, however, it solidifies in everyone's mind that there is a plan in place to hold on to what they have and to maintain it. That is the ultimate form of complacency, as it simply means everything is good enough and we don't want to expend effort. It is laziness, and that form of complacency ensures failure as effectively as any other.

Communities that adhere to the principal of sustainability where they truly embrace the status quo and just want to maintain what they have usually develop all sorts of plans and hire all sorts of consultants. Those consultants prepare wonderful documents full of generic strategies that are great for collecting dust on a shelf and, on occasion, being pulled off and displayed as evidence of the plan the community has in place for sustainability. In reality, thousands of communities around North America were created, and then grew, without consultants' plans and sustainability initiatives. The growth may not have been perfectly organized, or at times might have been a little haphazard, but the growth occurred nonetheless and usually did so because the attitude of the community was a progressive one that sought to contribute something for the future, not simply maintain what they had.

Consultants can help you organize and design plans for how you want to grow and develop your community, much like house plans direct a contractor in constructing a house. Many homes have been built without plans. They may not be as pretty or well designed as a planned house, but they can be built nonetheless. Many house plans, once designed, go unrealized, however, if no one follows through on the construction. Once the plans for the house are designed the real work begins. That is the same case for communities. The real work comes after the plans are designed. If home contractors worked the same as many communities do, however, they would sit around the job site waiting for the walls to jump up by themselves, or for someone to wander in and just start assembling them. Many communities hire a consultant, do up a plan for sustainability, and then sit and wait for everything to magically appear by itself.

Communities either spiral up or they spiral down. A spiral down can begin with the closing of just one business. It may not seem like too much of an issue at first, but the closing of that business means that a few people who worked there are now unemployed. No, actually it means that a few families in the community are now unemployed. That means they may have to move away to another place in order to find a job. If that occurs there are fewer children in your school, fewer people using your hospital, fewer volunteers for your service clubs, fewer people to donate to community causes, and less money spent in town. Everything adds up, and can lead to another business, perhaps already teetering on the brink, finally having to close its doors. That means a few more people without jobs in your community. Now there are a few more families without sufficient income. That means they may have to move to find work. That means fewer children in your school, fewer people using your hospital, fewer volunteers for your service clubs, fewer people to donate to community causes, and less money spent in town. That can lead to another business closing and ... I think you get the picture. The community enters a downward spiral.

The other scenario is that your community can spiral up. That means that a new business opens up which can now hire a few people in town who did not have a job before, so they don't have to move, or a few new people move to town because of those new jobs. No, actually their families come with them, which means there are more students in your school, more people utilizing your hospital, more volunteers for your service clubs, more people able to donate to community causes, and more money spent in town. More people and more money mean that another business might open, which employs a few more people who didn't have a job, or people from out of town who move to your community for the job. And of course their families come with them to the community, which means there are more students in your school, more people utilizing your hospital, more volunteers for your service clubs, more people able to donate to community causes, and more money spent in town. In other words, success breeds more success and your community enters an upward spiral.

For much of its first 60 years of existence, Omegatown was a bustling town of almost 2,000 people that had everything going for it. There was ample opportunity for entrepreneurs, with rail, road and runway connecting it to the world, lots of industry, a strong agricultural base, and plenty of businesses. Somewhere in those first 60 years, however, a sense of complacency overwhelmed it, a sense that it could never lose, never fail, and that prosperity would just naturally come to it. As such it maintained its population, its industry, and its connections as a matter more of good fortune than effort. The community just wanted to maintain itself, and they thought they would always be sustainable. The world changed, however. The world changed and transitioned as the community took for granted it could always remain the same. Businesses left, industry left, the railway left, people left. The town's population diminished to less than 1,000 while those around it grew. It didn't happen overnight, but rather was a slow and steady downward spiral that occurred over two decades.

Omegatown decided it needed to do something so they hired a consultant and created a sustainability plan. Yes, all would be better now. But it wasn't. A local developer decided to build a housing project that would serve the needs of the aging population so that fewer seniors would choose to leave for some other place that would provide them with housing that they desired. It was the largest building project in the community's history.

For years the project was held up, however, because people were afraid to lose their view of the golf course, or they didn't like the nature of the project, or it didn't fit their vision of what the project should be for seniors, or they didn't want it built in that location, or any number of other reasons. The project was even criticized by the local paper. Eventually it was completed because the local resident who proposed it was more determined to see it through than its opponents were to stop it. But it was the last development project to occur in that community – no other developers would consider it because of its reputation for obstructiveness, despite its sustainability plan.

The community was, and still is, on a slow downward spiral. They have their sustainability plan, but I don't believe anyone has read or followed it since it was first drafted. Their notion of being sustainable is to stay the same. No one wants to see anything change. They don't want to see people leave, the railway leave, businesses close, or industry move, but they oppose new developments, they fail to support new businesses, they overtax everything and everyone, and then they wonder why they spiral down. There are at least five locally owned businesses in the last two years in that small town that have closed their doors or have been sold to large conglomerates that take their profit out of town. The owners have sold their houses and moved away because the taxes are too high and the town administration makes opening another business or building another house too expensive, troublesome and time consuming. The irony is that everyone I talked to in that town as I did research feared desperately that the school and hospital would close because there were fewer students in the school and fewer patients in the hospital so they couldn't keep doctors in town. The sad part was that they thought it was everyone else's fault but theirs.

Omegatown, just like similar communities across North America, hired an economic development officer to help encourage growth and reverse the spiral. The type of person hired to be the economic development officer is itself a very telling sign of the commitment of a community. In fact, if I were an investor considering placing my money into a particular community, I would spend a few hours over supper with the EDO. In many communities this person is a local resident who is being paid a paltry sum but working the job full time. Invariably he (or she) is grossly under-qualified for the position, knows nothing about economic development, has no real understanding of how business works, and has little if any authority with anyone else in town to make decisions or accommodate your business needs. What happens most frequently in situations like this is nothing – nothing really happens and nothing is meant to happen. It is a move designed to create the illusion of action while complacency carries on. Many of these economic development officers get no support, no control, and no resources. The expectation seems to be that by simply hiring someone with the title of EDO, every business in the world will suddenly want to locate in that community. If that were the case all the communities, and there are a lot of them, that hired economic development officers would be doing much better than those that don't have them. That is simply not the case. In reality, the attitudes in the community have a greater correlation to its level of success than the existence of an economic development officer. So, in cases like this I would run like hell.

On occasion the economic development officer is a local business person who in fact does understand business and is serving as initial-contact person for prospective new businesses. This can sometimes be a better scenario, but on occasion that business person may secretly be protecting their own agenda (see Chapter 2, "Don't Attract Business") and can cost you tremendous time, energy and money and all the while may be obstructing progress on your investment. There is no way to know in advance if this is actually the case in any particular situation because some of those local business owners truly do understand that your success means their success and they may genuinely want to help you. You may want to consider, however, that it may be an indication of the value the community places on attracting business when a part-time person is hired for the job. As well, despite the best and honest intentions of a part-time locally hired business person serving as the EDO, that local business person may still face challenges in persuading (let alone enforcing) local decision-makers and the community as a whole to take action on your behalf if the mindset and values of the community are indifferent or opposed.

Personally, I would be more inclined to approach a community that had an economic development officer who was paid a good wage, worked the job full time, worked hand-in-hand with the town administrator, was listened to by his local authorities, and was not a local resident but rather had moved from another community to take the job. Why would I recommend that the EDO should be an outsider and not a native resident of the community? Simply because such a person is more likely to be a professional who is qualified for the position – if he didn't have these qualifications, he probably wouldn't have been offered the job. If the EDO moved from somewhere else, works closely with administrators and authorities and is listened to by them, then the person in all likelihood is legitimate and effective, and the community is probably displaying a true commitment to success rather than complacency. In contrast, a resident who is native to the community is more likely to have implicit conflicts of interest through loyalties to relatives or friends living there. In preference to this, I would probably seek out a community that didn't have an EDO at all. Then at least the responsibility of development has been internalized and you can judge for yourself whether or not the community is truly open to development and growth or whether the community and its members are determined to bring about their own failure.

It is not just small and medium-size communities that are prey to the threat of complacency, however. Many large cities have taken for granted that they are the hub of a large industry and that the industry will always be there and everything will be the same way it has always been. The community fails to adapt or respond to changing circumstances until it has become a virtual wasteland. Others assume that they have a competitive advantage that will ensure they are always the head office capital, banking centre, or preferred port of the nation and do little to fight to maintain their competitive advantage. There are numerous cities that have lost focus on what made them competitive and gradually, or suddenly, they have lost incredible amounts of ground and are falling behind other cities that have raced right past them. A city may have the seat of government, the seat of banking, the majority of corporate head offices, the best port, the best recreation, a concentration of industry, the best arts and culture, the best university, or any other factor, but if they are so convinced their competitive advantage makes them unbeatable, then their attitude of complacency will surely bring about their downturn as quickly and as drastically as it does for any other community.

We've all experienced complacency at some point in our lives. It may be at work or in our relationships. At work, if you become complacent it means the quality of your work will suffer, and you may lose that job or chance of advancement. In relationships, complacency means you quit calling to see how friends are doing, you quit buying flowers or giving kisses to the one you love. In both cases it usually means you have lost interest in your work, your spouse, or your friends. In a community, becoming complacent means the community members have lost interest in their own success. And even if the community itself fails to perceive this, others can see it clearly and will not look to that community as a place to raise a family and invest in. If you become complacent at work you have become complicit in the end of your own career. If you become complacent in your own relationships you have become complicit in the end of those relationships. Becoming complacent about the future of your community is a great way to kill it. If you become complacent about the future of your community then you are complicit in its end, and you bear the responsibility.

Chapter 13
Don't Take Responsibility

There are many ways to kill your community, to ensure its ultimate failure over the long term. I have emphasized consistently that this set of 13 Ways is not an exhaustive list. I am sure that everyone who is determined to keep their community from growing and prospering in the future and for future generations can come up with many more ways to kill a community that you have personally witnessed being put into action. I have also stood firm that successfully killing your community does not require the coordination and implementation of all these different methods – any one of these ways is powerful enough to cause the downfall of your community all by itself. Of this list of 13 Ways to Kill your Community, and any others you may add from your personal experiences, none is more powerful than the 13th Way.

The particular effectiveness of the "avoiding responsibility" technique is that it is contagious. It is like a game of hot potato: you take the potato – that is, the responsibility – gingerly, then quickly toss it to the next recipient before you feel the heat. Similarly, when someone feels the heat that comes from being quickly tossed the responsibility of a problem and finding its solution, the reaction is often to pass on the heat to someone else as quickly as possible.

The result is that responsibility is quickly passed around, and is accepted by nobody. You can witness this in coffee shop banter as people discuss all the things that are wrong with the community, or the school, or the church, or the committee, or the country, and talk about all the people and decisions that caused the problem to arise, but never contribute a solution or stand up and declare a desire to fix it. That would defeat the purpose of the game. That would take away the fun of tossing and deflecting the hot potato of responsibility around the room. People who aren't present are blamed for problems they didn't create and for implementing solutions that may not have worked. Even worse, it's often the people doing the blaming who are themselves part of the problem – but nary a one will contribute a hand or seek a solution to resolving the issue. That is such an exciting and powerful way to kill your community.

Even if others in your community have engaged the youth, seniors and immigrants, even if they have assessed your community's needs, taken risks, cooperated and tried new ideas, stopped living in the past, and improved your community by painting and improving the water situation, all is not yet lost. If you just make sure that you take no responsibility for your actions you will find others will begin to do the same. They will begin to blame others as they sit back and ridicule and scold and blame those who are trying so hard to build your community. Together, with that attitude that you bear no responsibility to act, you will turn your community in the right direction towards failure as more and more give up the fight and join you in blaming someone else for all that is wrong. If you can manage to do only one thing right to kill your community, not taking responsibility is the key.

Over the course of being an elected representative, I hear frequently from people bringing my attention to a wide range of issues, but sometimes I simply get a call from someone who just wants to complain. The worst call I ever received as a politician was from a gentleman, and I'll call him that loosely, who lashed out and criticized everyone and everything. At the time, cattle were blocked from crossing the border between the U.S. and Canada due to a single case of bovine spongiform encephalopathy (BSE) being discovered in Canada. All truck and trade in beef ceased even though the meat from that cow never entered the food system, borders were closed to cattle exports for some time. Millions of dollars were lost in Alberta and cattle farmers were getting rid of their cows at a record rate. I could understand his frustration. Trucking companies were unable to ship cattle to the U.S., so many of them had to lay off truck drivers, sell off trucks, or diversify what they hauled. Naturally, when the borders re-opened, the reverse problem emerged. As the cattle industry began to rebuild there was a greater and greater need for cattle liners and truck drives, but the cattle hauling industry did not respond instantly to the re-vitalization in the cattle industry, so there was a considerable period during which it was tough to find a cattle liner or truck driver to haul cattle anywhere.

During our conversation I couldn't get a word in while the gentleman just continued to rant and rave, using words I had obviously heard before, but never in such a flamboyant combination. There was no limit to his grievances. His community was lacking volunteers and it was the provincial government's fault. The national government was not adequately dealing with the Quebec issue, and he was mad about that too. He even insulted my grandfather, whom he had known years earlier. Before I could answer even one of his concerns, but as soon as he had run out of things to complain about, he hung up. The root of what I was hearing was that he couldn't make enough money and there wasn't enough work on the farm to support his son, and he complained that he couldn't find any truck drivers to haul his cattle.

It sounded to me as though he had two problems, each of which could be a solution to the other. Not having enough income and work on the farm to keep his son on the farm was a problem. His son would need another job. Hmmmmmmm. He couldn't find any truck drivers or trucks to haul his cattle, and if every rancher in the nation was in the same boat .... Hmmmmmmm. I love it when crisis meets opportunity, but I love it even better when two crises meet and are each other's opportunities.

Positive-thinking people see a problem and turn it into an opportunity. Those are the types of people that accept responsibility for their own destiny, they accept their ability to affect their own outcomes and to make good things happen, and they believe in their own talents and skills. Negative-thinking people take an opportunity and find a problem in it. They take a silver lining and find the dark cloud. They often hate the world, hate themselves, hate what life has delivered them and blame everyone and everything else for what happens to them and others – but never once do they accept that whatever negative outcome has befallen them, they themselves could turn it around if only they had the will and attitude. Alas, the attitude we have, and the understanding that often that attitude is the only thing we can control in our lives, and that we can control it from the moment we wake up to the moment we fall asleep, is the hardest thing to grasp and an almost impossible concept to accept.

For my caller this was an opportunity missed – all he could see was impossible challenges and a need for someone else to fix his problems. It was everyone else's fault, for everything that had gone wrong in his life. That was the attitude that would eventually lose him the farm, and his wife, and his friends, and his son. As he continued to blame those around him, fewer people stayed around him, which meant those that remained bore more and more of the blame. Eventually he sat alone in misery, a failed man. The larger lesson? That the refusal to accept responsibility and always blame someone else won't merely assist you to fail in life, but is also the right attitude if you want to kill your community. Simply assure yourself that "it" is not ever your fault – that it is the mayor's fault, the county council's fault, the chamber's fault, the grade three teacher's fault, the baseball coach's fault, the preacher's fault, the closing of the border, the problem with international relations, the Premier's or Prime Minister's fault. It doesn't matter, as long as you cast blame and responsibility to anyone but yourself. If you do that successfully then you can convince yourself and everyone else around you that all the problems you and your community face are their responsibility to deal with and you can wash your hands of the situation and go back to the coffee shop and complain.

There are so many Omegatown stories about responsibility being avoided and blame being assigned that an entire book could be written about that issue alone. No doubt, this is one of the most effective community-killing methods available. Many of the other techniques for killing your community require tremendous dedication and active effort, and – worst of all – may sometimes create a sense of guilt in the perpetrators that weakens their will to follow through and their commitment to their goal of destruction. The beauty of the "responsibility-avoiding" destruction method is that a sense of guilt, almost by definition, does not happen because the nature of this method is to assign guilt to someone else. Proper concentration on the task at hand, in fact, can lead the perpetrator to feel that they are truly just and right and trying to get action and resolution on some matter. Let us look at some examples.

In Omegatown a long standing issue was a shortage of housing that was suitable for seniors. I was invited to give my "13 Ways" speech by a group that declared it was dedicated to building seniors-appropriate housing in the community. I arrived early and did a tour of the community, visited town and county councillors, met with local business people, had coffee with seniors in a couple of different places, and finally met with the group of five people who were leading the charge in building seniors housing. They seemed very pleased to have me, and as always I was very excited to be there. I mentioned to them that it is rare that the people who actually need the speech ever show up to hear it but that I would listen and try to ensure the right message was delivered that evening. They told me about how there was a serious shortage of seniors housing in the community. They were angry at the lack of help they received from the municipal government, they were angry that their provincial representative had not helped them acquire seniors housing, and they were very upset the province had not already built seniors housing in their community. I listened closely and prepared my notes for the evening.

When I talked about the "13th Way" to kill your community I spoke directly to that group and explained what they were doing wrong. They were noble in their pursuit to acquire seniors-appropriate housing – but they were wrong on every other front. The wanted seniors housing, but they couldn't explain what type they were pursuing. It seemed to me that they wanted free housing in condominium-style developments with full, free healthcare and home care services for anyone over age 65. That simply doesn't exist, I explained, so expending futile effort, and extending blame when no action was taken on something that simply doesn't exist, was a distraction from the real issue, and actually prevented action from being taken. The group of five actually opposed a private contractor who built a condominium complex for older adults who were still very active but who wanted less sidewalk to shovel and lawn to mow. They actually wrote in the paper that they were opposed to the complex because it was not what "they" wanted. Nevertheless, the complex sold out and adult couples in the community were very excited to finally have "appropriate" housing for their needs and their age within their community.

The group of five also had cast blame on the local elected officials for inaction in moving them closer to their goal. They explained that for years the town officials had provided no assistance in actually moving the desired project ahead. I had discovered, however, that two of the five had actually served on the elected council for years and had themselves paid a consultant a huge sum of money to write a community profile report from which needs could be assessed. Over those years not one application for a grant had been submitted to build the project that (they claimed) they and the seniors so urgently wanted. In fact, I pointed out, the group had expended, and were still expending, all their effort and letter-writing in criticizing the local and regional politicians for allegedly doing nothing – even though the members of the group of five were themselves the ones who could and should have been formulating a plan and applying for the grants. They were not working for seniors housing projects, but rather had focused their efforts on demanding seniors housing from people who had no control on whether or not it was built. The single first step in building what they said they wanted was for them to take action, but they focused their energies on blaming anyone and everyone else for their own inaction. They were the epitome of the 13th Way, and I was very excited to have people hear the speech who really needed to hear the speech. Needless to say they were a little shocked and significantly appalled.

In another Omegatown case, the entire community, lead by the local doctor, had grown concerned over the future of their healthcare facility. They had read the rural development report I had written that outlined how healthcare, education, economic development and community infrastructure were the four cornerstones of a community. They asked that I come to their community to deliver the "13 Ways" speech, anticipating that it would point out the importance of healthcare to the community and how outside forces must not reduce or eliminate their local healthcare facilities. As always I did my due diligence, spoke to members of the community, interviewed everyone I could who was associated with the issue, and showed up to speak that evening. Everyone expected me to confirm their belief about how important the health facility was to the community and how it was critical that those who had the power to shut it down be forced not to shut it down. The problems that led to the potential closing of the facility (as it turned out there was absolutely no discussion of closing the health facility, but there should have been) had been created long before.

The local physician enjoyed his private practice in his local hospital. He was the lone physician in a large facility, which meant that he had exclusive access to the lab, and x-ray, and all other medical facilities there. Other physicians approached the community and the physician about adding a practice but the local physician always fought against any addition because, he argued to the community, there were not enough patients to support a second physician's practice. The community accepted this argument and so for over a decade only one practice existed within the community and the hospital that served it. A little research indicated, however, that increasing numbers of locals were driving up to 45 minutes to one of three neighbouring communities where numerous physicians served the populace.

Fewer and fewer locals went to their only local physician. Each had their reason. Perhaps there were personality conflicts, perhaps he wasn't very attentive to seniors, perhaps he wasn't very gentle with children, perhaps women felt uncomfortable with him, perhaps men felt compromised by him. He obviously could not be all things to all people. This was an excellent example of the sort of situation described in Chapter 2: that competition gives us such benefits as quality, selection and service. When it comes to healthcare providers, including physicians, perhaps we value the selection and service that comes from a little competition. Without choice, and without improvements in service, we choose with our feet to go somewhere else to get our groceries, to get our hardware, to buy our vehicles, and to see our doctors. We all like options and we all like good service and whether we believe it or not, we make choices that we feel will get them for us, even in healthcare.

The community, the locally elected officials, the physician and nurses were all concerned that their health facility would be closed down. They knew that fewer patients were being seen, fewer people were using the health facility, and that the facility could be closed as a cost cutting measure. There hadn't been any discussion of it being closed, but instinctively they knew there was a potential problem and they wanted to be pre-emptive, so they asked me to speak about how critical it was to keep it open. I thought more people would be upset over the information I had gathered and the message I delivered, but they seemed to actually expect it – well, everyone that is but the physician. I explained that any persons who cast blame for the potential closing of the facility should first cast blame on themselves, for they had allowed the physician to acquire what in effect was exclusive access to the facilities of the hospital, and they had allowed him to grow complacent and provide a level of service that caused their own community members to go elsewhere for their healthcare needs.

The blame could be cast in the end on those who wrote the order to close the facility, but the real responsibility for remedying the situation lay in the hands of those who created the problem. The council and community members who supported the physician in keeping an exclusive practice had actively supported the development of the current situation, and only they could turn it around. Higher officials should not properly be blamed for closing a facility that is under-utilized, is incredible costly, and has a reputation for poor service. The quality of care, the level of service, and the options available to local people had to be changed, and then the facility would be more efficient, less costly, better utilized, and deliver better care. Who could close a facility like that?

There are so many examples from Omegatown where responsibility has been cast off and blame redirected to someone who often has no control over the situation and the choices that must be made. Always before a problem situation develops there are ample opportunities to change course and avoid delay, delusions, and ultimately disaster, but often it is so much easier to cast blame in another person's direction and assign them the responsibility for finding a solution to a problem that is out of their hands, and in all likelihood is of your own making. Adopting that attitude is the soundest assurance that the problem will not be fixed, and that nothing good will be done while you drift around with a clean conscience. It is critical that you find someone else to take the responsibility and the corresponding blame for the problem that is yours to fix. You don't even have to find the right person to blame, or someone that is even remotely associated with the problem. Blame the teacher, preacher, doctor, farmer, politician, hockey coach, business man. Blame your neighbour, street cleaner, president, volunteers or the kids who play street hockey down the road. It really doesn't matter whom you blame. The point and purpose is to find someone, anyone, and then you will be free and clear to carry on doing nothing to resolve the problems that need to be fixed, the problems that are right there in your field of view. If you do that successfully, you can kill your community and lay the responsibility for its death at someone else's feet.

Stepping back a moment to take a look at the big picture, it's clear that avoiding responsibility is the most effective of the 13 Ways to Kill Your Community. Even if you've made mistakes by engaging your youth, seniors and immigrants, even if you've assessed your needs, you've taken risks, cooperated and tried new ideas, you've stopped living in the past, you've painted and improved your water quality, all is not yet lost – if you just make sure that you take no responsibility for your actions, that'll get you moving in the right direction. If you can manage to do only one thing right to kill your community, not taking responsibility is the key.

Conclusion

During the time it's taken you to read this book, I've had perhaps a hundred people tell me that the globe is urbanizing so there is no sense in working on rural development. "It is an impossible task." Or: "Your report that had 72 recommendations that cover health, education, community infrastructure, economic development, youth, seniors, aboriginals, immigrants, environment, water, transportation, arts and culture and so on is too large and will never get done." Or: "No one will act on it." Or: "Communities won't change their approach." Or: "There is no money." I simply smile at them.

Step by step we are making small changes, and I believe there will be a global community renewal that will begin in this decade and grow to a fever pitch within the next 20 years. It will take my next book to explain exactly why that will happen. In the meantime I will travel around speaking about what communities need to do to change their mindset in order to prepare for the growth that will come and even provide guidance on how to safeguard your community and ensure that growth is responsive for the future. I have travelled to hundreds of communities already and will go to hundreds more before my job is done. I've given the "13 Ways to Kill Your Community" speech hundreds of times to groups as large as 2,000 and as small as eight and I will continue to go where I am needed in the hope I can inspire change. I do this for my family, for my sons, and for the sons and daughters yet to come who deserve strong, sound communities to grow up in.

Just like the students whom I spoke about in the Introduction, creating change is about attitudes. Once those students understood that they were taking the first steps in destroying their own lives by smoking that joint at lunch or by not bothering to study for that math test, they had to stop and take notice of what they were doing. Once they could see that they were unintentionally harming their futures, they realized they would have to take steps to reverse that attitude and work in a more positive way to ensure a successful life. The same is to be said of communities.

The reason why rural development hasn't happened is because of wrong attitudes. Every one of the 13 Ways is about attitude. Out of all the things that affect our lives every day, we can really only control one, and that is our attitude. With the wrong attitude we can bring about our end very quickly. With the right attitude we can accomplish almost anything. Our biggest challenge is that our wealth has made us complacent and we have not had to work together to build as we have in the past. We are independent people who do not need a community for the same reason, namely for survival, as we did in the past, and so we have lost our sense of how to hold our community together. As a result our attitudes have strayed from community-building. Perhaps our attitudes have become completely counter to community-building. In the end, however, we cannot look to anyone but ourselves for the responsibility and the solutions.

There's a quote that says, "Whether you think you can, or you think you can't, you're right." Every day things pop up that can directly affect our goals, our dreams and ambitions. Every morning

13 Ways to Kill Your Community

when we wake up, we have only to choose if we want to succeed or fail, we have only to assess our values and adjust our behaviour, we have only to decide we can, and we can.

Attitude is the reason why a community fails, attitude will also be why a community will succeed. The wonderful thing about attitude is that it doesn't take staff, money and infrastructure. Attitude also can be pretty much changed overnight, which means that the first brick laid in the path to success is a change in attitude. Rural development will happen. It takes time and effort, obviously. Rural communities across North America can be successful with resourceful people who don't fall into the traps of the 13 Ways to Kill Your Community.

Whether it's making sure there is quality water in your community; engaging your youth, seniors or outsiders; assessing your needs and values; not becoming complacent; not being afraid to try new things; painting and keeping your town attractive; attracting business; cooperating; not living in the past; not being short-sighted; and of course taking responsibility in and for your community – if you can face all these challenges and overcome them, then you can avoid the pitfalls and traps that kill communities.

You will face opposition, you will face criticism, and you will face those who are desperate to prove you wrong. I faced them all when they said, and still say, that rural development is impossible. Don't let them upset you. Don't let them distract you. Don't let them grind you down. Simply do as I do. When they tell you that what you are doing is impossible, that it can't be done, simply look them in the eye and smile and reply:

"Those who say it cannot be done should not interrupt those who are doing it."

And if all else fails … give me a call.

Doug Griffiths was born and raised on a ranch just outside Coronation, Alberta. During university he worked on pipeline crews, as a custom pesticide applicator, and in a lumber yard before receiving an Honours Bachelor of Arts Degree in Philosophy and a Bachelor of Education Degree. He went on to teach for several years in the small community of Byemoor, Alberta, and was nominated for the Edwin Parr Beginning Teacher of the Year Award and twice for the Pan Canadian teaching award. During this period he also continued to ranch with his family.

Concern over the state of rural communities prompted Doug to seek election to the Alberta Legislative Assembly; he has won three elections and is currently serving as an MLA, representing Battle River-Wainwright. Doug most enjoys spending time with his family, teaching, and riding his horse; he now also travels far and wide to speak and consult on rural development and deliver his speech, "13 Ways to Kill Your Community."

Mr. Griffiths currently lives in Hardisty, a small community in east-central Alberta that was the subject of session 1 of the CBC series "The Week the Women Went." His wife, Sue, and their two boys, Austin (born December 2005) and Brady (born August 2008) love the community, the country, and rural Alberta life.

Kelly Clemmer is the editor-in-chief with Star News Inc. in Wainwright, Alberta. Kelly has been in the newspaper business for over 11 years, writes fiction and creates art in his spare time. Kelly is involved in organizing events and promoting the community of Wainwright and is one of the founding members of the Wainwright Arts Council. He lives in Wainwright with his wife Shannon and son Ashton.